Praise for *Without Roots*

"A sweeping analysis of the fundamental problem facing Europe, and an equally sweeping outline of the solution."

—National Review Online

"Ratzinger's discussion of the continent's religious and secular history is provocative, and his high regard for the American tradition of separation of church and state may also come as a surprise."

—Commonweal

"[N]o answer can be achieved if the roots of the debate are not fleshed out, and no answer will be of use to Western civilization without some steadfast statesmen who are willing to take up the responsibility of defending those roots—which may involve resorting to arms. That a pontiff and a leading Italian statesmen would jointly offer such sentiments may be a beneficial, if tardy, step in attacking Europe's sordid flirtation with politically correct platitudes."

—Weekly Standard

"A small, potent book ... An engrossing, enlightening, extremely timely discussion."

—Booklist

"These polemicists are feisty thinkers ... Sure to spark controversy, their manifesto is required reading for any student of comparative religion or Vatican politics ... Sharp intellect in service of moral vision."

—Kirkus Reviews

"A fascinating book."

—Charlotte Observer

"It has a quality of inviting the reader to join in the arguments, not accepting the ideas of pope and professor as dogma, but inviting scrutiny, beginning a search.... The Cardinal has a gift of making some opaque ideas—the kind that don't get debated too often in the marketplace, but should—transparently accessible. As he ranges though history, his comparisons of Europe and the United States alone justify reading this little book."

—Embassy Magazine

WITHOUT ROOTS

The West, Relativism,
Christianity, Islam

JOSEPH RATZINGER
NOW POPE BENEDICT XVI

MARCELLO PERA

Foreword by George Weigel

Translated by Michael F. Moore

BASIC
BOOKS

A Member of the Perseus Books Group
New York

Copyright © 2006 by Arnoldo Mondadori Editore S.p.A

Translation copyright © 2006 by Michael F. Moore

Hardcover published in 2006 by Basic Books
A Member of the Perseus Books Group
Paperback published in 2007 by Basic Books

Design by Jane Raese
Text set in 12 point Berthold Caslon

Cataloging-in-Publication Data for this book
is available from the Library of Congress.

ISBN-13: 978-0-465-00634-2
ISBN-10: 0-465-00634-5
Paperback ISBN-13: 978-0-465-00627-4
Paperback ISBN-10: 0-465-00627-2

10 9 8 7 6 5 4 3 2 1

Contents

Foreword

WHAT DRIVES HISTORY? Politics? Economics? Some combination of politics and economics? Or should we look elsewhere to find the engine of history–to the realm of the human spirit, perhaps? Might it be that culture–what men and women honor, cherish, and worship–is the most dynamic element in human affairs, at least over the long haul?

What is a civilization? Can we understand "European civilization," for example, simply by looking at its artifacts–what Europe "makes," technologically, agriculturally, and aesthetically? Or is that merely "civilization" on the surface? Might the sources of the civilization we call "Europe" be found in a distinctive encounter with, and a distinctive idea of, the sacred?

Indeed, is it possible to imagine anything properly called "civilization" that lacks a sense of the sacred?

These are some of the large questions explored in great intellectual depth in this small book, the result of a dialogue between Professor Marcello Pera, a philosopher and politician, and Cardinal Joseph Ratzinger—at the time of their exchange, the Prefect of the Vatican's Congregation for the Doctrine of the Faith, now Pope Benedict XVI. *Without Roots* was a stimulating exploration of the current state and future prospects of Europe when it was first published in Italy in 2004. Now, with Cardinal Ratzinger's election as the 264th successor of St. Peter, *Without Roots* takes on a new life, as a window into the mind of a pope who was elected, in part, because of his long experience with, and profound understanding of, the current crisis of European civilization.

"Crisis" is an overused word these days, but in the present circumstances of Europe it is, unfortunately, appropriate. Europe, Joseph Ratzinger writes, has become hollowed out from within, paralyzed in its culture and its public life by a "failure of its circulatory system." And the results of that hollowing-out are most evident in the unprecedented way in which Europe is depopulating itself. Generation after generation of below-replacement-level birthrates have created a demographic vacuum which, like all other vacuums in nature, is not remaining unfilled: the vacuum is being filled by transplanted populations whose presence in Europe is a challenge to Europe's identity, and could become a threat to European democracy.

What is happening when an entire continent, healthier, wealthier, and more secure than ever before, fails to create the human future in the most elemental sense–by creating future generations? There are obvious sociological and economic factors affecting Europe's demographic decline; might there be spiritual factors at play, too? Could Europe's disinclination to create the future have something to do with an apostasy toward the past–toward the spiritual roots of European civilization? And could that apostasy eventually threaten Europe's commitments to human rights, to equality before the law, to tolerance and civility among peoples of diverse convictions? Is it possible to sustain public commitments to those public goods on purely utilitarian grounds–because civility and tolerance "work better"? How can we speak of, and defend, "universal human rights" in a cultural climate in which the very idea of "truth" is under sustained assault?

These are some of the questions implied by the dialogue between Cardinal Ratzinger and Professor Pera–and these are some of the questions that Pope Benedict XVI will likely be raising during his pontificate. The questions are of urgent importance on both sides of the Atlantic Ocean. The American "culture war" is, in fact, an ongoing debate—and a continuing political struggle—between those who believe that human beings can, however inadequately, grasp the truth of how we ought to live together, and those for whom any notion of transcendent "truth" involves an unacceptable "imposition" of someone's "values" on someone else. Europe's exponents of a thoroughly secularized public space have their counterparts in the United States (and, it seems, have seized the cultural and political initiative in Canada). Thus, the issues explored so carefully by Cardinal Ratzinger and Professor Pera have everything to do with the future of North American democratic culture, as well as with the future of Europe.

George Weigel

Preface

THIS BOOK WAS BORN from a personal encounter. After the lecture that I gave at the Pontifical Lateran University on May 12, 2004, Cardinal Ratzinger gave his own lecture the next day in the Capital Room of the Italian Senate. This juxtaposition of the two speeches was purely by chance. As we discovered immediately after reading each other's talks and in the private meetings that followed, however, there was nothing casual about the often complete coincidence–arrived at independently and from very different perspectives–that we found in our concerns about the spiritual, cultural, and political situation of the West, and particularly of Europe today, and also about the causes of the situation and the primarily cultural remedies that could improve it.

Hence was born the idea for this book. It brings together the two lectures–my own in a revised and longer version than the brief text I delivered at the

Pontifical Lateran University—with the addition of a direct exchange of letters between us in which each tries to understand the other's reasons, clarify his own, and compare them with those of a broader public.

It is up to the readers to decide whether our intention—to examine and reflect on the great issues of our time, including the West, Europe, Christianity, Islam, war, and bioethical questions—has achieved its goal. Whether our concerns can be addressed. And whether our suggestions deserve to be pursued.

We hope that these pages will help to pierce the curtain of reticence and timidity that impedes discussion of our destiny today. The only thing worse than living without roots is struggling to get by without a future.

WITHOUT ROOTS

Relativism, Christianity, and the West

MARCELLO PERA

A Symptom

At the beginning of his famous essay, *The Protestant Ethic and the Spirit of Capitalism*, Max Weber raised the following question: "A product of modern European civilization, studying any problem of universal history, is bound to ask himself to what combination of circumstances the fact should be attributed that in Western civilization, and in Western civilization only, cultural phenomena have appeared which (as we like to think) lie in a line of development having *universal* significance and value."[1]

Weber was speaking in particular about "the most fateful force in our modern life, capitalism," but the same question might be asked of quite a few institutions not included on his list. Modern science, for example, is a Western invention that has a universal value. So, too, are liberalism, separation of civil society and state or church and state, the rule of law, the welfare state, democracy, as well as the "universal" conventions, declarations, and bills of rights. These and other institutions originate in and are characteristic of the West, particularly Western Europe. They belong to specific periods of Western history, have spread and imposed themselves in other parts of the world, and claim to have universal value.

The explanations that have been offered for these unique phenomena diverge, sometimes markedly. I will not enter into the merits of the solutions, although I feel obliged to mention that no serious attempt to account for these great moments in history has ignored the contribution of Christianity–direct or indirect, causal or concomitant, determinant or auxiliary, supportive or critical–thereby confirming that Christianity has been the greatest force in Western history. Instead I wish to focus on a new and paradoxical fact.

While the explanations have varied widely, the basic validity of the question has always been upheld. Today, by contrast, exactly one hundred years after the publication of Weber's essay, the *question* itself is the first thing to be questioned, criticized, and ultimately refuted. The thinking that currently prevails in the West regarding the universal features of the West is that none of them has universal value. According to the proponents of these ideas, the universality of Western institutions is an illusion, because in reality they are only one particularity among many, with a dignity equal to that of others, and without any intrinsic value superior to that of others. Consequently to recommend these institutions as universal would be a gesture of intellectual arrogance or an attempt at cultural hegemony, imposed by arms, politics, economics, or propaganda. Moreover it only goes to follow that seeking to export these same institutions to cultures or traditions that are different from our own would be an act of imperialism.

Samuel Huntington summarized this widespread Western trend in his celebrated book, more reviled than read, on the clash of civilizations. He summarizes his political thesis as follows: "In the emerging world of ethnic conflict and civilizational clash, Western belief in the universality of Western culture suffers three problems: it is false; it is immoral; and it is dangerous."[2]

One case in point is the question of "exporting" democracy. This issue has been the subject of extensive debate in relation to the second Iraq war and the "Greater Middle East" initiative launched by the President of the United States, George W. Bush. Opponents of these two initiatives have argued that democracy should not be exported. They do so not because the social, economic, legal, and institutional conditions of the countries affected are still backward, which would make the entire operation *premature*. Not because the institutions typical of democracy– the vote, equality, laws, parliaments, courts, and so forth–inevitably undergo sometimes profound modifications when they are grafted to different cultures (from England to India, for example, or from France to Algeria), which would make the operation *unilateral*. Instead they argue that exporting democracy would amount to imposing one form of life on other equally legitimate, worthy, respectable forms of life, which would make the operation *violent*.

One particularly revealing symptom shows the extent to which this mixture of timidity, prudence, convenience, reluctance, and fear has penetrated the fiber of the West. I refer to the form of self-censorship and self-repression that goes by the name of political correctness. "P.C." is the newspeak that the West uses nowadays to imply, allude to, or insinuate rather than to affirm or maintain.

We read and hear this newspeak every day. According to its dictates, everything can be compared and evaluated *within* the confines of Western culture—be it Coca-Cola with Chianti, Gaudí with Le Corbusier, Darwinism with intelligent design—and many comparisons can be made *between* aspects of Western culture and their counterparts in other cultures, such as hospitality, social customs, individual behavior, clothing, and so forth. Yet should one attempt to place in a hierarchical order these cultures or civilizations—such as the ones that Max Weber described in the past and Samuel Huntington describes in the present—or to simply organize them according to a scale of preferences, from better to worse, out pop self-censorship, prohibitions, and linguistic restraints. Consequently, as one can easily document in today's newspeak, whenever a culture lacks or flatly rejects our institutions, we are not allowed to say that our own culture is *better* or simply *preferable*. The only thing that politeness allows us to say is that cultures and civilizations are *different*.

To me this form of linguistic re-education is unacceptable. I reject it on moral grounds, which are the ultimate reason for refuting an intellectual position.[3]

To justify this rejection, I will outline my argument in the following manner.

First, by way of introduction, I will refer to a concrete application of newspeak: our relationship with Islam. Then I will move from the political symptom to the cultural cause, and attempt to refute this cause–relativism–in the two philosophical embodiments of relativism that the West has served up for many years now. Finally I will examine three practical consequences of this philosophy: the negative influence of post-conciliar relativism on Christian theology, which helps to explain the current weakness of the Church and the failure to obtain recognition of the Christian roots of Europe in the new (and now defunct) European Constitutional Treaty; the malaise of Europe, a rich continent that is unsure of its identity and its future and powerless to solve the resulting problems; and finally, the West's boredom with its own principles and values, at the very moment in which it has been targeted by a deadly war declared and conducted by Islamic fundamentalism.

The world is filled with concern but also with hypocrisy. Hypocrisy on the part of people who see no evil and speak no evil to avoid becoming involved; who see no evil and speak no evil to avoid appearing rude; who proclaim half-truths and imply the rest, to avoid assuming responsibility. These are the paralyzing consequences of the "political" correctness (as well as intellectual, cultural, and linguistic correctness) that I reject. Of course I may be wrong. Indeed, I would like to think that my worst fears stem from a faulty analysis of the situation. If this were so, all I would need to know is that these fears have helped something or someone.

The Double Paralysis of the West

After years of virtual or remote anthropology exercises conducted by philosophers and scientists to prove that cultures cannot be arranged in hierarchical order, the case of Islam is finally real, at hand, and ever present.

In 1992, a French expert on Islam, Olivier Roy, wrote that "Political Islam cannot resist the test of power. . . . Islamism has been transformed into a neo-fundamentalism that cares only about re-establishing Islamic law, the *sharia*, without inventing new political forms."[4] As proof, he pointed to a long list of shortcomings and failures. Islam has not produced its own political model, economic system, autonomous public institutions, division between the family and the state, equal rights for women, or community of states founded on anything except religion. In other words, he considered Islam a failure. Rather than open itself up to new prospects, "The Islamic parenthesis has closed a door, the door of the revolution and the Islamic state."[5]

I wonder whether the thesis of Olivier Roy, and of so many Westerners who are thinking along the same lines, is true or false.[6] If it is true, can one then say that the Western model is better than the Islamic one?

The response to the first question depends solely on empirical research and analysis. The response to the second question does not, mainly because it patently expresses an evaluation ("better"). At this point, it would be useful to make a preliminary distinction: the difference between making a judgment and making a decision; in other words, the difference between affirming a thesis—in this case a value thesis of the type "A is better than B"—and taking a stand, in this case a political stand of the type "follow A," "fight against B." The two questions are related, although not in a logical, deductive manner. To argue that the model of Western democratic institutions and rights is better than the Islamic model does not imply taking any particular course of action. One could say that the West is better than Islam and still tolerate Islam, respect Islam, dialogue with Islam, ignore Islam, or even obstruct Islam, clash with Islam, among the many possible stances. According to the old proverb, it's one thing to say, another to do. To rephrase this proposition in logical terms, there are no formal implications between "is" and "ought" (*ab esse ad oportere non valet consequentia*, as one says in Latin).

The dominant culture in the West, however, thinks the opposite, and reveals its prejudices through a major flaw in reasoning. It thinks that "ought" descends from "is." According to this way of thinking, if a person maintains that the West *is* better than Islam—or, to be more specific, that democracy is better than theocracy, a liberal constitution better than *sharia*, a parliamentary decision better than a *sura*, a civil society better than an *umma*, a sentence by an independent tribunal better than a *fatwa*, citizenship better than *dhimma*, and so forth—then he or she *ought* to clash with Islam. This is an error of logic that compounds the error of believing that our institutions have no right or basis to be proclaimed as universal.[7]

The consequence of these two errors is that today the West is paralyzed twice over. It is paralyzed because it does not believe that there are good reasons to say that it is better than Islam. And it is paralyzed because it believes that, if such reasons do indeed exist, then the West would have to fight Islam.

I personally reject these positions. I deny that there are no valid reasons for comparing and judging institutions, principles, and values. I deny that such a comparison cannot conclude that Western institutions are better than their Islamic counterparts. And I deny that a comparison will necessarily give rise to a conflict. I do not deny, however, that if an offer to dialogue is responded to with a conflict, then the conflict should not be accepted. For me the opposite holds true. I affirm the principles of tolerance, peaceful coexistence, and respect that are characteristic of the West today. However, if someone refuses to reciprocate these principles and declares hostility or a *jihad* against us, I believe that we must acknowledge that this person is our adversary. In short, I reject the self-censorship of the West. This self-censorship—much more than the universalist claims of Western institutions critiqued by Huntington—is something that I find unjustified and dangerous.

The Relativism of the Contextualists

Let me begin by stating unequivocally that the cultural critique of universalism has no solid grounds.

The notion that the judgment of cultures or civilizations constitutes an invalid mode of inquiry has been put forward, most notoriously, by the school of thought known as relativism. Various names have been given to this school today: post-enlightenment thinking, post-modernism, "weak thought,"[8] deconstructionism. The labels have changed, but the target is always the same: to proclaim that there are no grounds for our values and no solid proof or argument establishing that any one thing is better or more valid than another.

Relativism stems from an irrefutable fact, the existence of a plurality of values, and from a hardly refutable position, that it is impossible for all values to coexist. There is always a circumstance in which the pursuit of one value, such as friendship, is incompatible with the pursuit of another, such as justice. A typical example of such a conflict is when a friend commits a crime before our eyes: should we violate the friendship by reporting the friend to the police, or should we keep the friendship by denying the truth and becoming accomplices? From such premises, relativism derives erroneous and disastrous consequences, in particular, the conclusion that sets of values, such as cultures and civilizations, cannot be judged by comparison to one another.

Two main lines of reasoning are generally adopted in support of this conclusion. The first is that cultures, theories, conceptual universes, language games, or worldviews—depending on the methods or terminology used—cannot be measured in terms of each other. The second is that certain concepts are intrinsically paradoxical ("aporetic," to use the technical term), especially concepts that are related to values, such as state, democracy, and faith.

The best-known example of the first approach is Wittgenstein's *Philosophical Investigations*. His thesis is that the meaning of a term is contingent upon the use that is made of it in a language ("meaning *is* use"), and that every linguistic universe has its own rules of construction, signification, and decision.[9] The basic argument in support of his thesis is that contents cannot be separated from the criteria by which they are judged. What one community holds to be true, beautiful, and good is only so according to the criteria by which that community defines them. The criteria are always *infra-* rather than *inter-*

cultural. There are no meta-criteria that can establish intrinsic truth, absolute beauty, or universal good. All criteria, according to this line of reasoning, are contextual.

In my critique of this thesis, I will limit myself to observing that a judgment of whether culture A is better than culture B does not require a meta-criterion that is common to both A and B. The only thing required is that the members of A and B wish to enter into a dialogue and submit to each other's criticism. In the midst or at the conclusion of a dialogue, one interlocutor will run into difficulty defending himself to the other. This does not mean that the thesis of the latter will automatically be true. (Since truth is a semantic property of sentences, it cannot be defined according to the epistemic criteria governing them.) However, it will certainly be the better position. Better in the only concrete meaning that has been granted to mortals to know. Better because it stands up to criticism, objections, and denials. Better epistemically, if the context of the dialogue is cognitive. Better axiologically, if the context is values. Better politically, if the context is politics.

Some might object that what I am proposing is the old dialectical method of *elenchos*[10]–refutation or cross-examination–used by Gorgias, Socrates, Plato, and Aristotle. They would therefore consider the method to be valid only *within* a specific culture, namely Western culture. There are many possible replies, but the decisive proof is as follows. If the members of culture B freely demonstrate their preference for culture A and not vice versa—if, for example, migration flows move from Islamic countries to Western countries and not vice versa—then there is indeed reason to believe that A is better than B.

Others might object that the latter proposition is false, because the conversion (or migration) of B to A could be the result of indoctrination, propaganda, or error. I would answer them by saying, "If you, a contextual relativist belonging to culture A, speak of *error*, you are contradicting yourself, because to recognize an error within culture B, A and B would have to share a common criterion for 'error' that makes it possible to distinguish between the real and the apparent in *both* cultures." But if there is indeed a criterion common to two cultures, then the relativism of the contextualists collapses. Their relativism has developed such an appetite for the foundations of other doctrines that, in the end, having devoured everything else, it becomes self-destructive and devours itself.

The Relativism of the Deconstructionists

This same self-destruction underlies the other approach taken by relativism, namely deconstruction, which according to most accounts was founded by the German philosopher Friedrich Nietzsche.

The deconstructionist operates by using the technique of exposing the loopholes, or *aporia*, in concepts that are supposedly absolute or universal. Another name for this technique is unmasking, or reversal, in which concepts transposed to extreme situations outside the purview of their normal use reveal the shape of their semantic ambiguity.

The acknowledged master of this technique is the French philosopher Jacques Derrida. He applied deconstruction to a series of fundamental Western concepts to prove that they could not pass the test of their supposed universality. For example, he deconstructed hospitality, to show that it is a form of imposition. He deconstructed democracy, to conclude that it is an exercise of force. He deconstructed the state, to show that the state, per se, is a rogue. Ultimately he ventured into today's most controversial exercise: to deconstruct terrorism.

To illustrate Derrida's technique–but also to prepare the reader–let us consider the case of hospitality, a concept that is relevant to contemporary immigration policies.[11]

Derrida takes as his starting point the correct observation that when hospitality is offered to a foreigner, he should be protected, even if his culture is strange to us. The best way to do so, it would seem, is to grant him the protection of our laws, first by teaching him the language in which our laws are written, the customs in which they are embedded, and the traditions in which they are entrenched. In short, the best way to offer hospitality to a foreigner is to integrate him into our culture. But the very concept of integration, of conditional acceptance, proves to be paradoxical. The foreigner ends up being treated not as a *he* but as a *we,* and he is offered hospitality by the same measure in which he ceases to be a foreigner.

On the other hand, let us consider the foreigner precisely as a *he.* In other words, let us accept him unconditionally. Upon careful reflection, the unconditional acceptance of the foreigner violates the most elementary rules of hospitality, because accepting another person as a *he* without at the same time respecting our own *we* destroys the very assumptions on which hospitality is founded. This, too, is paradoxical.

What is Derrida's conclusion? Integration, this wonderful concept so beloved by the liberal West, is really a form of imposition. And what about dialogue, tolerance, respect, and reciprocal offers to meet and learn from and about each other? Derrida does not address these concepts, presumably because they, too, could be deconstructed.

This is an intelligent conclusion, no doubt, and also an amusing, but sadly impoverished, intellectual game. Why does Derrida never reach the point of stating that a *value choice*—in favor of dialogue, tolerance, and so forth—is the ultimate basis for an intellectual or political position? Perhaps because, due to an almost imperceptible platonic reflex, he believes the opposite, namely (and here he is mistaken) that if the foundations of hospitality are unknowable, then one can neither be hospitable nor apply integration policies. I can only wonder whether "deconstructionist" is simply another name for a disillusioned Platonist.

Let us consider another argument, again by way of example: the deconstruction of democracy. Derrida examines a case that has been cited a thousand times: "The fascist and Nazi totalitarianisms have come to power as a result of electoral dynamics that, from a formal point of view, are considered normal and democratic." He asks, "Should a democracy grant freedom to those who might attack democratic freedoms and put them in a position to exercise their power and put an end to democratic freedom for the sake of democracy and the majority of votes that they might be able to get?"[12]

But why, one might ask, should democracy, which is a classic axiological concept, be defined "from a formal point of view"? Once again, Derrida fails to make a value choice that would define democracy in terms that are anything other than the ordinary procedural business of vote counting. Of the term "democracy," he says that "it contains an essence without essence and without object."[13] But this brings us back to the earlier platonic syndrome: Derrida seems to think that if this essence does not exist, then it is also not worth fighting to defend democracy ("if God is dead, everything is allowed, isn't it?"). In either case, deconstruction operates at a price that transforms philosophy into a careless, gratuitous exercise and the philosopher into a concept-cleaner who isn't even required to punch in (on the time-clock of responsibility for his own moral decisions).

Now that we have seen how this technique works, let us return to Derrida's general deconstructionist doctrine. What has been gained through the cumulative efforts of so many deconstructionists?

If what remains is doubt over the existence of solid definitive or ultimate foundations of the concepts (or worse, of the "essences") of hospitality, democracy, the state, and so on, then there has been a net gain, although it is a reward that was already known at the outset. People no longer believe in "ultimate" foundations; they no longer dream of essences. If what remains instead is the inability or impotence to act, then there has been an unequivocal loss: only philosophers in their classrooms can afford the luxury of not taking practical decisions; not so the man of the street, the politician, the head of state. Moreoever, if, on the other hand, one hopes to learn a line of behavior or a course of action from deconstruction, then out jumps a contradiction.

Derrida himself paid the price. Confronted by the terrorist attacks of September 11, he first began to deconstruct them ("We do not in fact know what we are saying or naming in this way: September 11, *le 11 septembre*, 9/11"). Then, since he could no longer avoid the issue of how to fight terrorism, he appealed—as did so many others—to the United Nations. He wrote, "It is thus necessary to do everything possible (a formidable and imposing task for the very long term) to ensure that these current failings in the present state of these institutions are effectively sanctioned and, in truth, discouraged in advance by a new organization." Exactly like the United Nations, but "modified in its structure and charter," so that it can "have at its disposal an effective intervening force and thus no longer have to depend in order to carry out its decisions on rich and powerful, actually or virtually hegemonic, nation-states which bend the law in accordance with their force and according to their interests."[14]

An excellent idea. Except that an important detail is missing. How can a person appeal to an "international institution of law and an international court of justice"–and thus a democratic institution–after law, justice, and democracy have been deconstructed? Even the most daring deconstructionist will fall if he saws off the branch on which he is sitting.

To soften the blow, Derrida covers his fall. He concedes that his "unity of force and law ... is not only utopic but *aporetic*," and adds, "I continue to believe that it is faith in the possibility of this impossible and, in truth, undecidable thing ... that must govern all our decisions."[15]

You heard right: *faith*. In the end, the true answer comes out, but it is the same exact answer you would have heard from a poor, maligned, and much deconstructed enlightenment philosopher with his back up against the wall. In other words, Derrida returns to the starting point, the value choice, from which all else derives. What an amusing, tortuous philosophers' maze is deconstruction.

Relativism, no matter how true its premises may be, rests on shaky foundations. Contextualism and deconstruction have the *facts* against them. In opposing contextualism, I do not deny the relationship between criteria and contents (a typical mutual reinforcement). What I deny is the thesis of Paul Feyerabend that "Every theory has its own experience," or of Thomas Kuhn that "The proponents of competing paradigms practice their trades in different worlds."[16] In opposing deconstruction, I do not deny that facts cannot exist independently of their interpretation. What I deny are the theses of Nietzsche that "There are no facts [*Tatsachen*], only interpretations," and of Derrida, "There is nothing outside the text."[17]

On the contrary, facts and elements "outside the text" do indeed exist. They may not be hard facts or indestructible ramparts, but they are a fundamental and often decisive element for our arguments to prove or disprove a thesis. To oppose scientific relativism, one can assert the *facts of experience*; ultimately, not even the staunchest Ptolemaic could deny that the planet Venus has its phases. To oppose cultural relativism, one can counter with the *facts of expectations*. Ultimately, not even Derrida denies that, to confront terrorism, most people expect a decision from international organizations. And to oppose civilizational relativism, one can counter with the *fact of preferences*. Ultimately, not even the most ardent multicultural relativist would deny that all human beings, given the choice, prefer to live in conditions of security, respect, health, prosperity, and peace.

What remains in the end is moral faith–to which even Derrida ultimately appeals–or religious faith. However, what if this, too, were relative? If Christianity, too, were not an achievement with universal value, but merely a culture with neither more nor less merit than many others? This is another characteristic of the way the West feels today, a characteristic on which we would do well to reflect.

The Relativism of the Theologians

Joseph Cardinal Ratzinger wrote that "Relativism . . . in certain respects has become the real religion of modern man," and that it "is the most profound difficulty of our day."[18] Then he raised a series of questions: "The power of Christianity, which made it into a world religion, consisted in its synthesis of reason, faith, and life. ... [W]hy is this synthesis no longer convincing today? Why, on the contrary, are enlightenment and Christianity regarded today as contradicting each other and even mutually exclusive? What has changed in the enlightenment, or in Christianity, that it should be so?"[19]

In the case of rationality, I think I am qualified to respond. What has changed is our belief in the foundations, proofs, justifications, and good reasons. In the case of Christianity I dare say that what has changed is our sense of faith in Revelation.

Relativism has also begun to infiltrate, but has not yet expunged, Christian theology, the final stronghold, taking the place of both exclusiveness and inclusiveness. The takeover proceeded in the customary manner. The starting point was the phenomenological observation that there is a plurality of creeds and religions. This was followed by a comparison, a loss of hope in meta-criteria. The end point is doubt in fundamental creeds of Christianity (the final stage, the reinterpretation or deconstruction of the religious facts).

The theologian Paul Knitter takes a typical approach. "The fundamental premise of unitive pluralism," he wrote, "is that all religions are, or can be, equally valid. This means that their founders, the religious figures behind them, are or can be equally valid. But that would open up the possibility that Jesus Christ is 'one among many' in the world of saviors and revealers. Such a recognition, for the Christian, is simply not allowed. Or is it?"[20]

However unprecedented it may be for a Christian, according to Knitter, he *can* indeed make such an acknowledgment. This is how several theologians, including John Hick and himself, sought to revise the fundamental—and universal—points of traditional Christology. *Ego sum via, veritas et vita*—"I am the way, the truth, and the life." *Extra Verbum nulla salus*—"There is no other name in which we shall find salvation." Jesus is the only begotten Son of God. These and other affirmations in the Gospels, relativist theologians would have us believe, should be revised or understood differently. How? By contextualizing or deconstructing them.

Knitter writes, "In talking about Jesus, the New Testament authors use the language not of analytic philosophers but rather of enthusiastic believers, not of scientists but of lovers." And if a believer says,

"Jesus is my only love," he should be understood, Knitter goes on to claim, the same way one would a husband saying to his wife, "You are the most beautiful woman in the world. . . . You are the only woman for me."[21] In short, saying, "Jesus, I love you," amounts to neither more nor less than saying, "Darling, I love you." Naturally the experts–namely the analytic philosophers and scholars–cannot use such an earthy language. Not even in the bedroom can they allow themselves such linguistic intimacies. They have to speak in a more educated, appropriate fashion. And since they are relativists, all they can do is to speak relativistically, relativizing even the figure of Jesus Christ.

However, why should the poor uneducated believer have to convert to the newspeak of expert analytical philosophers? The reason, as Cardinal Ratzinger wrote, is because, "The belief that there is indeed a truth, valid and binding within history itself, in the figure of Jesus Christ and in the faith of the Church, is referred to as fundamentalism."[22] And since fundamentalism is treated as the eighth deadly sin today, better to take the vow of relativism, especially since, as Ratzinger states, "Relativism thus also appears as being the philosophical basis of democracy."[23]

So the answer that the expert theologian provides to the uneducated believer would seem to be to engage in self-censorship. The believer in Christ cannot say that Christ is *the* truth, because that would be dogmatic and anti-historical. Nor can he or she say that Christ is the *sole* truth, because that would constitute fundamentalism.

Cardinal Ratzinger rejects this thesis, which I, too, find contradictory, false, and counterproductive for Christians. Contradictory, because if relativism leads us to claim that there are no basic truths, then not even relativism can be the foundation of democracy. False, because democracy places at its very foundations the values of the individual, dignity, equality, and respect. Deny these values and you deny democracy. Counterproductive, because if, relativistically speaking, one truth is equivalent to another, what is the purpose of dialogue? And if faith contains no truth, how can we be saved?

I believe that the notion of a relativist Christian is oxymoronic; it leads not to dialogue but to apostasy. It collapses at the same point where all relativisms collapse: when it treads on *facts,* or to be precise, on the "Christian fact," as the Patriarch of Venice, Angelo Cardinal Scola, has called it, which consists "in the decision of the transcendent Truth, the *Deus*

Trinitas, to communicate Himself to man in a form that is free, living, and personal."[24]

For the believer, Christ is the Revelation, the Truth, the Word become flesh, an individual, a Person.[25] For both the poor Christian, who professes and expresses the faith in his own way, and the educated philosopher or scholar, who analyzes and describes it in his, the Revelation of God as Man plays the same role as expectations, when cultures are compared, or preferences, when civilizations are compared: the role of fact. Either you deny this fact, and then affirm spiritual relativism, or you acknowledge it and prepare to accept the consequences.

Christianity, Dialogue, and Islam

What are the consequences of the Christian fact? Here I would like to move from a theoretical critique of relativism to an examination of what it entails.

For centuries, conversion to the Christian faith seems to have had a single effect: the affirmation that there is no salvation outside of Christ or "in any other name," the same expression that Knitter punctuates with a question mark. This exclusiveness has fallen into disuse today, however, and its place has been taken by an inclusiveness often associated with the need for dialogue embraced by the Second Vatican Council and post-conciliar theology. This openness to dialogue has raised questions of its own, in particular two: what is the *purpose* of this dialogue; and what is its *subject*?

Let us begin with the first question. In typical dialectical contexts—common, political, legal, aesthetic, and even epistemic conversations—dialogue is an instrument through which to discover or approach the truth. This is because dialogue uses the technique of cross-examination (*élenchos*) to uncover contradictions and minimize the margin of error. However, in religious contexts, at least in the context of Christian religion, dialogue cannot be an instrument for the discovery of truth, because Revelation plays that role. In other words, in Christianity truth is not a process but a *state*, not a becoming but a *being*.

Religious dialogue can therefore have two purposes: for believers of various faiths to communicate and to foster mutual understanding; and to preach, spread, and advance the message ("Go out into the world and preach the Gospel to every creature").

The first purpose does not cause any particular problems, aside from the cultural differences it encounters. If pursued, it fosters coexistence, tolerance, and respect among men of various religions and creeds. The same cannot be said of the second purpose, in which communication is amplified by *persuasion,* and comprehension by *evangelization.* What is the relationship between these two purposes?

This question became particularly vexing in light of the uncertainties left by Vatican II, especially a certain submissiveness in post-conciliar debate and practice. It is still the source of dispute, clarifications, corrections, and inquiries: a caution that is justified by the sensitive nature of the issue of coexistence among religions–especially in the age of relativism. However, not even the most sympathetic comprehension of the undertaking can disguise a sense of the difficulty or uncertainty that arises from Catholic doctrine today.

According to one encyclical, *Redemptoris missio,* "Inter-religious dialogue is part of the Church's evangelizing mission," and "dialogue does not dispense from evangelization" (article 55). What does it mean to be a "part of" that mission? Does it mean to be an *element* of it, as in the expression, "Mathematics is part of modern education"? Or does it mean to be an *instrument,* as in the expression, "Mathematics is part of modern physics"? The basic meaning would seem to be the second: dialogue is the instrument of the evangelizing mission. It regards the method of preaching, and, in this sense, it replaces other methods, such as indoctrination, imposition, or propaganda. So why doesn't the encyclical use the expression "instrument of evangelization," rather than the far weaker "method and means of mutual knowledge and enrichment"? Why doesn't it dispel the ambiguity between the words "element" and "instrument"?

This is not a purely linguistic question but rather a doctrinal one. I am thus inclined to think that the answer resides in two related fears: the fear, heightened by relativism, that dialogue as an instrument of evangelization will be perceived as a covert form of imperialism; and the fear that in some circumstances, evangelization could also lead to conflict.

Which brings me to the second question: what is the dialogue about? The same ambiguities and uncertainties persist. It should not be possible to answer this question with regard to contents, since for the believer there is no such thing as an interrogation or correction of mistakes. Revelation is the Truth. One could therefore reply that dialogue concerns such values as brotherhood, tolerance, peace, dignity, the promotion of the human person, emancipation, and justice, which are common to many religions.[26] But these are *secular* or *secularizing* values. Christian evangelism does not preach secularism but transcendence, the unique, sole, true transcendence. However, if this transcendence is unique, how can we talk about the existence of "elements of truth and grace" in other religions?[27] Moreover, if the Church preaches this transcendence, how can we speak of dialogue?

Father Piero Gheddo recently rose to the challenge set by an American sociologist, who had proposed an alliance between Christianity and Islam in the name of the same values that some quarters of Islam preach against the Christian West; primarily "Its fierce resistance to certain forms of accommodation with the Enlightenment, such as the privatization of religion and the 'wall of separation' between religion and the state, and its scorn for 'irreligious' or 'indifferent' agents of modernization."[28] Father Gheddo recalled that, "In no Islamic country are Christians totally free, unlike Muslims in the West. ... The Muslims should examine their own consciences with regard to their collective behavior: the systematic violation of human rights, terrorism, oppressive practices against women and children, the lack of democracy, religious and social formalism that crushes the individual."[29]

Unfortunately many Muslims are not searching their souls, and while we allow mosques to flourish right next-door to our parish churches, in almost no Muslim country are Christians allowed to build a church. Even worse, while Muslims do not accept reciprocity of our principles and values, we allow these same principles and values to be deconstructed relativistically, and we theorize dialogue even when, as Father Gheddo writes, "We should recognize that the dialogue conceived by the fathers of the Council has born little fruit."[30]

If the possibility of dialogue is cast into doubt, however, what should replace or assist it? This is a difficult issue for Christianity, especially if, after lending its ears to relativism, it seeks to take its distance from it. There is one risk: that the fear of making choices will lead Christians to think that if the burdens of Christianity are too heavy, then it is better to dilute the faith or lower one's voice rather than risk conflict. But a weak Christian, like a weak thinker, ultimately becomes an acquiescent Christian.

One can only hope that this is not the case. Christianity is so consubstantial to the West that any surrender on its part would have devastating consequences. Things have recently taken a new direction, and the voice of doctrine is once again being heard.

Although Pope John Paul II has often promoted inter-religious dialogue, he has also issued various statements that contained firm reminders of what constitutes the true Christian faith.[31] After the inevitable resistance and controversy that followed, will the Church, the clergy, and the faithful be able to and want to be purified of the relativism that has almost erased their identity and weakened their message and witness?

Europe without Roots

Optimism is obligatory, but it's cheap. In the current situation, there is a heavy price to pay. Relativism has wreaked havoc, and it continues to act as a mirror and an echo chamber for the dark mood that has fallen over the West. It has paralyzed the West, when it is already disoriented and at a standstill, rendered it defenseless when it is already acquiescent, and confused it when it is already reluctant to rise to the challenge.

One should not think of philosophy as a luxury for initiates, to be consumed only within the walls of the university. It is instead a powerful tool for the promotion and spread of ideas and energy, and a vehicle of influential opinions. It always has been. It would thus be mistaken to think that relativism has never hurt anyone, or that it has never steered anyone down the wrong path, or even that it represents the height of theoretical tolerance, political elegance, and philosophical refinement. The opposite instead is true.

Plato's *Republic* supports a strong, shrewd state. Descartes' *cogito ergo sum* leads to his provisional moral code. Marx's surplus-value is grounded in the class struggle. Hume's "association of ideas" is connected with the morality of sympathy and the liberal ethic. Croce's "dialectic of the distinct" is based on absolute freedom. Gentile's "pure act" leads to totalitarianism or permanent revolution. Popper's "conjectures and refutations" are linked to the open society, Nozick's minimum state leads to anarchy, and Rawls's "theory of justice" to liberal democracy. The list goes on. In the same way, the relativism that preaches the equivalence of values or cultures is grounded not so much in tolerance as in acquiescence, more inclined toward capitulation than awareness, more focused on decline than on the force of conviction, progress, and mission (which were once typical of Christianity, Europe, and the West).

Allow me to cite another example, which refers back to my discussion of theological relativism: the question of the Christian roots of Europe. When the proposal was made to insert a reference to the Christian roots of Europe in the preamble to the European Constitutional Treaty, it was rejected, for reasons that should give us food for thought.[32]

Pope John Paul II's personal commitment to this cause is well known. In 2004 he delivered a series of statements on the subject: "The identity of Europe would be incomprehensible without Christianity" (May 2); "You don't cut off the roots from which you were born" (June 20); and "May Europe be itself and come to terms with its Christian roots" (August 4). So important did he consider it that he devoted a long, detailed Apostolic Exhortation to the topic. The essence of his argument could be summed up in a single quotation: "The Christian faith has shaped the culture of the continent and is inextricably bound up with its history, to the extent that Europe's history would be incomprehensible without reference to the events which marked first the great period of evangelization and then the long centuries in which Christianity, despite the painful division between East and West, came to be the religion of the European peoples."[33]

Unfortunately, these words went unheeded, like a *vox clamantis in deserto,* a voice crying out in the wilderness. The proposal was rejected and the defeat was round. What is most disturbing is that it was accompanied not by a bang but a whimper. Not even the Church, in my opinion, rose to the challenge.

The reason for this half-heartedness is not because there is some truth to the proposition that Europe does not have Christian roots (or, to be more precise, Judeo-Christian roots). Or because our freedoms and our liberalism do not depend on the Christianity from which they are derived and to which they are bound.[34] On the contrary.[35]

It is true that almost all of the achievements that we consider most laudable are derived from Christianity or were influenced by Christianity, by the message of God become Man.

In truth, without this message, which has transformed all human beings into persons in the image of God, individuals would have no dignity.

In truth, our values, rights, and duties of equality, tolerance, respect, solidarity, and compassion are born from God's sacrifice.

In truth, our attitude toward others, toward all others, whatever their condition, class, appearance, or culture, is shaped by the Christian revolution.

In truth, even our institutions are inspired by Christianity, including the secular institutions of government that render unto Caesar that which is Caesar's. And the list goes on.[36]

So why then did this proposal fail and why were its proponents so feeble? Why was the Pope's insistent appeal ignored? My own explanation is that in the age of triumphant relativism and "silent apostasy," *belief in the true no longer exists: the mission of the true is considered fundamentalism, and the very affirmation of the true creates or raises fears.*[37]

If these opinions and sentiments have infiltrated Christian theology, if from the philosophy departments they have trickled down into the clergy and spread to the parishes and families in the apartment buildings next door, how can we hope that Christians will obtain for their faith the recognition that it deserves? How can we hope that the clergy and the Christian masses of Europe will mobilize on behalf of a faith that reminds them of their grave responsibilities, at the same time as they are being mobilized in favor of a peace that must be made and a dialogue that must be entertained with the very people who openly attack the fundamental values of the West and desire neither peace nor dialogue?

The fight to obtain recognition for the Christian roots of today's Europe has proved to be in vain. To give you one example, the theologian Gösta

Hallonsten asked, "In this process of unification, what role could be played by Christianity which, while inextricably linked with the historical identity of the European peoples, is nevertheless seen today more as old merchandise meant for exportation rather than as a specific product of the European market?"[38]

The role that it plays is, alas, a weak one. Relativism has debilitated our Christian defenses and prepared or inclined us for surrender. It has convinced us that there is nothing worth fighting for or risking. It does not even object when others attempt to remove the crucifix from our schools (this happened in Italy). It presumes to see itself at the foundations of the secular state while it actually changes (or deconstructs) into a secular state religion of the state that prohibits Muslim girls in a European country from wearing the *hijab* to school (this happened in France). It shirks the educational burden of true integration, and one fine day it decides to separate these same boys and girls of Islamic faith from other boys and girls in a scholastic ghetto (this also happened in Italy).

The New Spirit of Munich

The one left footing the bill for this relativist culture today is Europe, first and foremost. Two major failures indicate the price that Europe is paying: the replacement of the grand design of a European Constitution with a more modest Constitutional Treaty; and the fracturing of the Atlantic alliance in the lead-up to the war in Iraq.

The second failure helps to explain the first. The war in Iraq, which began on March 20, 2003, with the bombing of Baghdad, followed a doctrine that is explained at length in the National Security document released by the United States' administration on September 17, 2002. This doctrine is summarized in the letter of accompaniment from President George W. Bush.

The substance of his message is Wilsonian, in the sense that it resembles the doctrine illustrated by President Woodrow Wilson to the Paris Peace Conference of 1918, on two basic points, in particular. The first is opposition to relativism. Bush, like Wilson, is a believer in universal values: "People everywhere want to be able to speak freely; choose who will govern them; worship as they please; educate their children—male and female; own property; and enjoy the benefits of their labor. These values of freedom are right and true for every person, in every society—and the duty of protecting these values against their enemies is the common calling of freedom-loving people across the globe and across the ages."[39]

Notice the words, "everywhere," "for every person," "in every society," "across the globe," and "across the ages." Values are unique and common. In this universal vision of values and rights, there is no room for distinctions between peoples, cultures, and countries.

President Bush is also Wilsonian in his goals. He adopts the same triad—political freedom, economic freedom, and security. He starts with the main goal, peace: "Today, the international community has the best chance since the rise of the nation-state in the seventeenth century to build a world where great powers compete in peace instead of continually prepare for war." Then he names the specific goals: "We will actively work to bring the hope of democracy, development, free markets, and free trade to every corner of the world."[40]

However, this is where the resemblances end. Wilson took a utopian approach. He was facing the prospects of peace after a war that the United States had ended. Bush takes a belligerent approach. He is facing a war brought to American soil for which there is no end in sight: "Defending our Nation against its enemies is the first and fundamental commitment of the Federal Government." Since Wilson's time, war has changed, the enemies are invisible, and the terrorists are harbored by rogue states. "The gravest danger . . . lies at the crossroads of radicalism and technology." For Bush, this means that, "As a matter of common sense and self-defense, America will act against such emerging threats before they are fully formed." This is the doctrine of preventive war.[41]

Europe has not accepted this rationale. It applied its veto in the United Nations Security Council. It has split between those who participate in the Coalition of the Willing and those who do not, between those who send troops for reconstruction and security and those who refuse to do even that much. And it is rotting. It is rotting and crying out, with slogans of uneven persuasion but equal substance: "No war!" "No preventive war!" "No unilateral war!" "No war that has not been legitimated by international organizations!" The complaints of the intellectuals have reached a feverish pitch. The same figures who declared on September 11, 2001, "We are all

Americans," quickly changed their tune. The same figures who were deeply moved by the fatalities and rubble of the Twin Towers have suddenly become realistic, prudent, and hostile. Those who have always scattered to the wind the best, most humane sentiments are now claiming that America was asking for it, articulating self-flagellating theories for the West and a sympathetic understanding of the terrorists' motivations.

How did this come to pass?

Because Europe does not know where to begin looking for its identity, it cannot speak in a single voice, affirm a single strategy, or assert a single supranational or strategic interest—apart from the occasional pipe dream of local hegemony—on matters pertaining to its own faith and security.[42] Because Europe has made a flawed analysis of Islamic terrorism—based on an anti-American bias—in the mistaken belief that it is a limited and easily contained phenomenon. Because it believes that the terrorist war is an act of reaction rather than of aggression.[43] Because it has experienced and enjoyed peace for sixty years and is thus inclined to believe that peace is a natural state and a natural right, and that perpetual peace can indeed exist.[44] Because it is convinced that it is someone else's job to guarantee security. Because it thinks that to achieve peace no price is too high: not appeasement, not massacres on its own soil, not even surrender to terrorists. Because Europe is impotent, and "from its impotence it derives a principle."[45]

A foul wind is blowing through Europe. I am referring to the idea that all we have to do is wait and our troubles will disappear by themselves, so that we can afford to be lenient even with people who threaten us, and that in the end, everything will work out for the best. This same wind blew through Munich in 1938. While the wind might sound like a sigh of relief, it is really a shortness of breath. It could turn out to be the death-rattle of a continent that no longer understands what principles to believe, and consequently mixes everything together in a rhetorical hodgepodge. A continent whose population is decreasing. A continent whose economy cannot compete. A continent that does not invest in research. That thinks that the protective social state is an institution free of charge. That is unwilling to shoulder the responsibilities attendant upon its history and its role. That seeks to be a counterweight without carrying its own weight. That, when called upon to fight, always replies that fighting is the *extrema ratio*, as if to say that war is a *ratio* that should *never* be used.

While the West Slept

So why take the risk of fighting? Is there a war, perhaps? I answer yes, there is a war, and I believe that the responsible thing to do is to recognize it and to say so, regardless of whether the politically correct thing to do is to keep our mouths shut.[46]

In Afghanistan, Kashmir, Chechnya, Dagestan, Ossetia, the Philippines, Saudi Arabia, the Sudan, Bosnia, Kosovo, the Palestinian Territories, Egypt, Morocco, and much of the Islamic and Arab world, large groups of fundamentalists, radicals, extremists—the Taliban, Al Qaeda, Hezbollah, Hamas, the Muslim Brothers, Islamic Jihad, the Islamic Armed Group, and many more—have declared a holy war, *jihad*, on the West. This is not my imagination. It is a message they have proclaimed, written, communicated, preached, and circulated in black and white. Why should we not take note of it?

Some might say that it's not really a war: it is a conflict declared by certain minority groups. I answer no, even if it is "just" a conflict, it's still an armed conflict. Others might chime in that the acts of terrorism are being committed by a few fanatics. I answer no, terrorism is the instrument of a war that is being fought, and "a few" fanatics are, in reality, many, many terrorists. Finally, some people might object that we should not, in our turn, take up weapons to fight. I would answer that I sincerely hope that we do not have to, but why should we exclude the possibility a priori? If there is a war, and it is a just war waged in self-defense, would it not be permitted by Christianity? Has not Christianity waged similar wars in the not-so-distant past?

But do not misunderstand me, either deliberately or through distraction. I am *not* advocating a Western declaration of war or state of war. I am advocating something else that to me seems even more important. I am urging people to realize that a war has indeed been declared on the West. I am *not* pushing for a rejection of dialogue, which we need more than ever with those Islamic countries that wish to live in peaceful coexistence with the West, to our mutual benefit. I am asking for something more fundamental: I am asking for people to realize that dialogue will be a waste of time if one of the two partners to the dialogue states beforehand that one idea is as good as the other.

People do not realize these two things, or rather I see little or no evidence that they do, especially in Europe. Nor do I find them widespread in European

Christianity, especially among the clergy, who today are dumbfounded, dismayed, resigned, and too often either stridently opposed to what should really be their cultural standard or else just plain silent.

There is a deep reason for this lack of awareness that I can understand and respect. The idea of being the target of a war is frightening. But can we be so sure that fear will not strengthen the hand of the belligerents? Will that acquiescence pay off? Will that capitulation to blackmail not lead to further attempts at blackmail and further capitulations? Would it not be preferable and more useful to show ourselves firm and resolute in defense of our good reasons?

In addition to the many reasons that I know and understand, there is one reason that I do *not* understand: the notion of Western guilt. At its most basic level, guilt is nothing more than a mistake made yesterday, acknowledged today, and experienced hereafter with regret and remorse. The West is not all wine and roses, and it has committed many mistakes that it acknowledges today because of the consequences that they later generated. The West was the father of a great civilization, although it came at the high price of colonialism, imperialism, anti-Semitism, Nazism, fascism, and communism. These were huge mistakes. But yesterday's mistakes are no justification for inaction or for ignoring what is happening today. If we wish to present an accurate record, we must draw up two columns and place the rights in a column next to the wrongs, in the same way that if we wish to have a fair trial, we need to counter the accusation with a defense.

"Western civilization," according to the Italian writer Pietro Citati, "has its grave faults, like any human civilization. It has violated and destroyed continents and religions. But it has a talent that no other civilization has known: the talent of gathering, for at least two thousand years now—ever since the Greek goldsmiths worked for the Scythians—every tradition, every myth, and every religion or every or almost every human being."[47]

After denouncing the same faults, the Peruvian writer Mario Vargas Llosa stated of Western civilization, "Its most significant merit, which may constitute a singular achievement in the broad array of world cultures ... has been its ability to be self-critical."[48]

This same concept of error has also penetrated the Catholic Church, which with growing frequency today recognizes the wrongs it has done, its erroneous decisions, and its unjust choices. The Church has apologized for evangelizing missions that were not always free of violence. It has apologized to the Jews for accusing them of Deicide and for persecuting them. It has apologized to Galileo for putting him on trial. The list goes on. Laudable intentions and a commendable attitude, because the errors of yesterday must be recognized if they are to be avoided tomorrow. But there is a risk of sending mixed signals. If the Church draws a line between the infallible truth of its message and its historical practices, and between its roles as the eternal guardian of truth and as the government *pro tempore* of believers, then people might perceive it as no different from any other secular institution that corrects its course over time. Such a division would leave its followers wondering whether the demands made of them today will not instead be considered faults tomorrow.

The self-criticism described by Vargas Llosa is always useful. But why take it to such an extreme, in Europe and in America, with such self-condemnation, self-immolation, and atonement, combined with such scarce recognition of our great merits? I truly do not understand. Perhaps the West today no longer understands what is right. It only knows what is wrong, and it readjusts its notions of right and wrong every time that someone complains about one of its errors. Or maybe it is simply exhausted. As

Vargas Llosa has said, "Democracy is an event that provokes yawns in the countries in which rule of law exists."[49]

I hope that he's wrong, and that the lethargy he describes does not exist. But if, unfortunately, he is right, then we need to start rubbing our eyes and wake up.

The Spiritual Roots of Europe: Yesterday, Today, and Tomorrow

JOSEPH RATZINGER

The Rise of Europe

What is the true definition of Europe? This age-old question was raised by Józef Cardinal Glemp during discussions in one of the language groups of the Synod of Bishops for Europe. Where does Europe begin, and where does it end? Why, for example, is Siberia not considered part of Europe, although many Europeans also live there, and it has a wholly European style of thinking and living? To the south of the community of Russian peoples, where do the borders of Europe disappear? Where do its borders flow in the Atlantic? Which islands are European and which, instead, are not, and why not? In these discussions it became perfectly clear that Europe is a geographic term only in a secondary sense: Europe is not a continent that can be defined solely in geographic terms but is rather a cultural and historical concept.

Let us consider the origin of Europe. Experts traditionally trace it back to Herodotus (ca. 484–425 B.C.), the first known writer to designate Europe as a geographic concept, which he defines in the following manner: "For the Persians consider Asia and the barbarian peoples who live there as part of their property, while they maintain that Europe and the Greek world are a separate country."[1] While he does not indicate the borders of Europe, the lands at the heart of today's Europe were completely outside of the visual field of the ancient historian. In fact, the formation of the Hellenistic states and the Roman Empire led to the establishment of a "continent" that would become the basis for the later Europe, despite having completely different borders. As a whole, the lands facing the Mediterranean came to form a true continent by virtue of their cultural ties, trade routes, and common political system. It was not until the triumphal advance of Islam in the seventh and early eighth centuries that a border would be drawn across the Mediterranean, subdividing what had been a single continent into three: Asia, Africa, and Europe.

In the East, the ancient world was transformed more slowly than in the West. After transferring its capital to Constantinople, the Roman Empire would survive in the East until the fifteenth century, although it was pushed further and further to the margins.[2] During the same period, the southern Mediterranean region found itself cut off completely (in approximately A.D. 700) from what had been a cultural continent for centuries, while Europe grew steadily northward. The ancient continental border that the Romans called *limes* disappeared. A new historical space opened up whose heartland encompassed Gaul, Germany, and Britannia, and whose northern reach expanded more and more toward Scandinavia. Amid this process of shifting borders, a theology of history was constructed that guaranteed ideal continuity with the earlier Mediterranean continent in its various forms. According to this thinking, rooted in the Book of Daniel, the Roman Empire had been renewed and transformed by the Christian faith, which therefore became the last reign in the history of the world, the framework of peoples and states that became defined as the permanent "Sacrum Imperium Romanum," the Holy Roman Empire.

The process of forming a new historical and cultural identity took place in a fully conscious manner under the reign of Charlemagne, when the ancient name of Europe returned to circulation, but with a new meaning. It came to define the kingdom of Charlemagne and to express an awareness of both the continuity and the novelty of this new aggregate of states, which appeared as a force that had a great future. A great future because it could be perceived as a continuation of a world history that until then had been rooted in the permanent.[3] The awareness of a definitive nature and of a mission was expressed through the emerging sense of self-consciousness.

With the end of the Carolingian age, however, the concept of Europe virtually disappeared, surviving only in scholarly usage. The term did not become popular currency until the beginning of the modern era—as a means of self-identification, in response to the Turkish threat—when it was asserted more in general in the eighteenth century. Apart from the history of the name, the decisive step toward Europe as we understand it today was taken when the Frankish kingdom constituted itself as the heir to the Roman Empire, which had never completely faded.[4]

Nor should we forget the existence of a second, non-Western Europe. In Byzantium (which considered itself the true Rome), the Roman Empire had withstood the upheaval of migrations and the Islamic invasion. The Eastern Roman Empire had never declined, and it continued to advance claims on the Empire's Western half. It extended as far north as the Slavic world, and created its own Greco-Roman world that distinguished itself from the Latin Europe of the West by introducing variants in the liturgy and in the ecclesiastical constitution, adopting a different script, and renouncing the use of Latin as the common language.

The two worlds also had sufficient unifying elements, however, to be considered a single continent. First of all, both the East and the West were the heirs to the Bible and to the ancient Church, which in both worlds refer beyond themselves to an origin that lies outside of today's Europe, namely in Palestine. Second, both shared the idea of Empire and of the essential nature of the Church, and therefore of law and legal instruments. The last factor I would mention is monasticism, which throughout the great upheavals of history has continued to be the indispensable bearer not only of cultural continuity but above all of fundamental religious and moral values, the ultimate guidance of humankind. As a pre-political and supra-political force, monasticism was also the harbinger of ever welcome and necessary rebirths of culture and civilization.[5]

Alongside the common ecclesiastical inheritance of the two Europes, however, a profound difference remained whose importance has been explained particularly well by Endre von Ivánka. In Byzantium, Empire and Church were virtually identified in each other. The emperor was also the head of the Church. He considered himself a representative of Christ and—following the Biblical example of Melchizedek, who was both king and priest (Genesis 14:18)—he bore the official title "king and priest" from the sixth century on.[6] Once the Emperor Constantine had left Rome, the autonomous position of bishop of Rome—as successor to Peter and supreme pastor of the Church—could be transplanted to the ancient capital of the Empire, where a duality of powers had been established at the beginning of the Age of Constantine. Neither the emperor nor the pope was absolute: each had separate powers.

Pope Gelasius I (492–496) expressed his vision of the West in a famous letter to the Byzantine Emperor Anastasius I, and, more explicitly, in his fourth treatise, where, with reference to the Byzantine model of Melchizedek, he affirmed that the unity of powers lies exclusively in Christ: "As a matter of fact, because of human weakness (pride), He has separated the two offices for the time that followed, so that neither shall become proud" (chapter 11). On matters pertaining to eternal life, the Christian emperors need priests (*pontifices*), who in their turn should follow, on temporal matters, the orders of the emperor. On worldly matters, priests should follow the laws of the emperor installed by divine decree, while on divine matters the emperor should submit to the priest.[7] The fourth treatise introduced a separation and distinction of powers that would be of vital importance to the future development of Europe, and that laid the foundations for the distinguishing characteristics of the West.

Despite these restrictions, both sides continued to be driven to seek absolute power and to impose their power on the other, making the principle of separation also the source of endless strife. How this principle should be lived properly and how it should be concretized politically and religiously continue to be a fundamental issue in present and future Europe.

The Turning Point of the Modern Era

To summarize my preceding remarks, the European continent was born from the rise of the Carolingian Empire and the shift of the Roman Empire to Byzantium, which directed its mission toward the Slavic peoples. If we accept this premise, the beginning of the modern era marked a watershed, a radical change, for the two Europes both in the essence of the continent and its geographic outlines.

In 1453 Constantinople was conquered by the Turks. Otto Hiltbrunner describes the event laconically: "The last . . . learned men emigrated . . . to Italy and passed on their knowledge of the original Greek texts to the Renaissance humanists; but the East was overcome by the absence of culture."[8] This may be an overstatement, since the reign of the Osmanli dynasty had its own culture, too. However, the European, Greco-Christian culture of Byzantium did indeed come to an end. There was a risk that one of the two branches of Europe would disappear, but the Byzantine heritage did not die: Moscow declared itself to be the third Rome, and founded its patriarchate on the principle of a second *translatio imperii,* or transfer of political power. Russia thus emerged as a new metamorphosis of the Holy Roman Empire, as a distinct form of Europe, which nevertheless remained tied to the West and was increasingly oriented toward it, culminating in Peter the Great's attempt to westernize Russia.

This northward expansion of Byzantine Europe meant that the continent's borders also began to extend toward the East. While the selection of the Urals as the border may have been exceedingly arbitrary, the world to the east of the Urals became a kind of substructure of Europe, neither Asian nor European, that was substantially forged by the European subject at the same time as it was excluded from having subject status itself. It became the object rather than the architect of its own history, not unlike a colonial state.

At the beginning of the modern era, two events took place that lie at the foundations of non-Western, Byzantine Europe: the breakup of ancient Byzantium and of its historical continuity with the Roman Empire; and the establishment of a second Europe, with a new capital in Moscow, whose borders extended eastward, and a type of pre-colonial structure in Siberia.

During the same period, two events of major historical significance also took place in the West. The first is that most of the Germanic world broke away from Rome. The rise of a new, "enlightened" form of Christianity drew a separation line through the "West" that clearly marked not just a geographical but also a cultural *limes,* a border between two different ways of thinking and relating. Within the Protestant world, there was also a rupture in the first instance between the Lutherans and the Reformed communities, to which the Methodists and Presbyterians belonged. At the same time, the Anglican Church tried to steer a middle course between Catholics and Evangelicals. These divisions were later amplified by the difference between Christianity as a form of state religion, which came to be a European hallmark, and the free churches, which, as we shall see, would make their home in North America.

The second event was the discovery of the Americas. The eastward expansion of Europe, through the progressive expansion of Russia into Asia, corresponded to a radical expansion of Europe beyond its own geographic borders to a world on the other side of the ocean that was given the name "America." The subdivision of Europe into a Latin Catholic half and a Germanic Protestant half came to be reflected in the part of the New World occupied by Europe. At first America was perceived as an outpost of Europe, a colony. In the wake of the French Revolution and the upheaval it sparked in Europe, however, America took on the characteristics of a subject. From the nineteenth century on, although America had been intimately shaped by its European birth, it became an independent subject in its dealings with Europe.

In the attempt to know the deepest, innermost identity of Europe through the study of its history, we have dwelled on two watershed moments in its history. The first came about through the confluence of three factors: the breakup of the ancient Mediterranean continent by the Holy Roman Empire, which was then relocated further north; the emergence of Europe as a Latin-Western territory during the Carolingian period; and the transference of the ancient Roman Empire to Byzantium, which expanded northward in its turn into the Slavic world. The second turning point was the fall of Byzantium, which came about in part through the northward shift of Europe, the eastward shift of the Christian idea of Empire, and the internal division of Europe into two separate worlds, Germanic Protestant and Latin Catholic (which was replicated in the Americas and would remain even after the new continent had established itself as a historical subject on a par with Europe).

Let us now turn to the third watershed, which was brought about by the French Revolution. Although the Holy Roman Empire had been in decline since the late Middle Ages, and it had faded also as a valid, undisputed interpretation of history, it was not until the French Revolution that the spiritual framework which it provided—and without which Europe could not have been formed—would shatter in a formal sense. This process had a major impact on both politics and ideals. In terms of ideals, there was a rejection of the sacred foundation both of history and of the state. History was no longer measured on the basis of an idea of God that had preceded and molded it. The state came to be understood in purely secular terms, as grounded in rationalism and the will of the citizens.

The secular state arose for the first time in history, abandoning and excluding as mythological any divine guarantee or legitimation of the political element, and declaring that God is a private question that does not belong to the public sphere or to the democratic formation of the public will. Public life came to be considered the domain of reason alone, which had no place for a seemingly unknowable God: from this perspective, religion and faith in God belonged to the domain of sentiment, not of reason. God and His will therefore ceased to be relevant to public life.

In the late eighteenth and early nineteenth centuries, a new schism thus developed whose gravity we are only now grasping. There is no word for this schism in German, because in Germany it emerged very slowly. The romance languages, by contrast, define it as a division between *Cattolici* and *laici*.[9] Over the past two centuries, a deep rift has opened between the two groups in the Latin nations. Protestant Christianity, by contrast, was initially able to accommodate liberal, enlightenment ideas without jeopardizing the framework of a broad Christian consensus. The ancient idea of Empire was shattered by the formation of powerful nation-states–defined by their distinctive linguistic spheres–which proved to be the true bearers of history. In the place of Empire there was a plural historical subject, the great European nations, whose drama was that each considered itself the depository of a universal mission, creating potential conflicts whose fatal impact we have experienced so painfully in the century that has just elapsed.

The Universalization of European Culture and the Ensuing Crisis

We must now consider the process by which this history of past centuries was transmitted to new worlds. The two halves of ancient pre-modern Europe had essentially known only one next-door neighbor, with whom it had to negotiate as a matter of life and death: namely, the Islamic world. It was only a question of time before Europe would expand toward America and in part toward Asia, continents that were lacking in great cultural protagonists. Still later, Europe would begin to make further incursions into these two continents, Africa and Asia, which it had previously dealt with only marginally, and which it would seek to transform into European franchises, into colonies.

If colonization could be considered a success, it is in the sense that contemporary Asia and Africa can also pursue the ideal of a world shaped by technology and prosperity. Yet there, too, the ancient religious traditions are undergoing a crisis, and secular thinking has made inroads and begun to dominate public life.

These processes have also produced the opposite effect: Islam has been reborn, in part because of the new material wealth acquired by the Islamic countries, but mainly because of people's conviction that Islam can provide a valid spiritual foundation to their lives. Such a foundation seems to have eluded old Europe, which, despite its enduring political and economic power, seems to be on the road to decline and fall.

By contrast to Europe's denial of its religious and moral foundations, Asia's great religious traditions—especially the mystical component expressed in Buddhism—have been elevated as spiritual powers. The optimism in European culture that Arnold Toynbee could still voice in the early fifties sounds strangely antiquated today: "We are faced by the fact that, of the twenty-one civilizations that have been born alive and have proceeded to grow, thirteen are dead and buried; that seven of the remaining eight are apparently in decline; and that the eighth, which is our own, may also have passed its zenith."[10] Who would repeat these same words today? Above all, what is European culture, and what has remained of it? Is European culture perhaps nothing more than the technology and trade civilization that has marched triumphantly across the planet? Or is it instead a post-European culture born on the ruins of the ancient European cultures?

There is a paradoxical synchrony in these developments. The victory of the post-European techno-secular world and the universalization of its lifestyle and thinking have spread the impression—especially in the non-European countries of Asia and Africa—that Europe's value system, culture, and faith—in other words, the very foundations of its identity—have reached the end of the road, and have indeed already departed from the scene. From this perspective, the time has apparently arrived to affirm the value systems of other worlds, such as pre-Colombian America, Islam, or Asian mysticism.

At the hour of its greatest success, Europe seems hollow, as if it were internally paralyzed by a failure of its circulatory system that is endangering its life, subjecting it to transplants that erase its identity. At the same time as its sustaining spiritual forces have collapsed, a growing decline in its ethnicity is also taking place.

Europe is infected by a strange lack of desire for the future. Children, our future, are perceived as a threat to the present, as if they were taking something away from our lives. Children are seen as a liability rather than as a source of hope. There is a clear comparison between today's situation and the decline of the Roman Empire. In its final days, Rome still functioned as a great historical framework, but in practice it was already subsisting on models that were destined to fail. Its vital energy had been depleted.

Now let us turn to the problems of the present. There are two opposing diagnoses on the possible future of Europe. On the one hand, there is the thesis of Oswald Spengler, who believed that he had identified a natural law for the great moments in cultural history: first came the birth of a culture, then its gradual rise, flourishing, slow decline, aging, and death. Spengler argued his thesis with ample documentation, culled from the history of cultures, that demonstrated the law of the natural life cycle. His thesis was that the West would come to an end, and that it was rushing heedlessly toward its demise, despite every effort to stop it. Europe could of course bequeath its gifts to a new emerging culture–following the example set by previous cultures during their decline–but as a historical subject its life cycle had effectively ended.

Spengler's "biologistic" thesis attracted fierce opponents during the period between the two wars, especially in Catholic circles. Arnold Toynbee reserved harsh words for it, in arguments too readily ignored today.[11] Toynbee emphasized the difference between technological-material progress and true progress, which he defined as spiritualization. He recognized that the Western world was indeed undergoing a crisis, which he attributed to the abandonment of religion for the cult of technology, nationalism, and militarism. For him this crisis had a name: secularism.

If you know the cause of an illness, you can also find a cure: the religious heritage in all its forms had to be reintroduced, especially the "heritage of Western Christianity."[12] Rather than a biologistic vision, he offers a voluntaristic one focused on the energy of creative minorities and exceptional individuals.

This leads us to the question of whether Toynbee's diagnosis is correct. If it is, then we must ask whether it is in our power to reintroduce the religious dimension through a synthesis of residual Christianity and the religious heritage of humankind. The Spengler-Toynbee debate remains open because we cannot see into the future. Nevertheless it is our duty to ask which factors will guarantee the future and which have allowed the inner identity of Europe to survive throughout its metamorphoses in history. To put it more simply, what can still promise, today and tomorrow, to offer human dignity to life?

To find an answer we must once again survey the present situation and its historical roots. We had gone as far as the French Revolution and the nineteenth century. Since that time, two new European models have developed. In the Latin nations the secular model has prevailed. A sharp distinction is made between the state and the religious bodies, deeming the latter to fall under the private sphere. The state denies that it has a religious foundation and affirms that it is based on reason and rational knowledge. Since reason is inherently fragile, however, these secular systems have proved to be weak, becoming easy targets for dictatorships. They survive only because elements of the old moral conscience have persevered, even without the earlier foundations, enabling the existence of a basic moral consensus.

In the Germanic world, the liberal Protestant model of church and state has prevailed. An enlightened and essentially moral Christian religion has some forms of worship that are supported by the state. This relationship guarantees a moral consensus and a broad religious foundation to which individual non-state religions must adapt. This model has long guaranteed state and social cohesion in Great Britain, the Scandinavian states, and once upon a time also in Prussian-dominated Germany. In Germany, however, the collapse of Prussian State Christianity left a vacuum that would later provide fertile soil for a dictatorship. Today state churches throughout the world are characterized by their fatigue. Moral force–the foundation on which to build–does not emanate from either the religious bodies subservient to the state nor from the state itself.

Situated between the two models is the one adopted by the United States of America. Built on the foundations created by the free churches, it adopts a rigid dogma of separation between church and state. Above and beyond the single denominations, it is characterized by a Protestant Christian consensus that is not defined in denominational terms, but rather in association with the country's sense of a special religious mission toward the rest of the world. The religious sphere thus acquires a significant weight in public affairs and emerges as a pre-political and supra-political force with the potential to have a decisive impact on political life. Of course, one cannot hide the fact that in the United States, also, the Christian heritage is falling apart at an incessant pace, while at the same time the rapid increase in the Hispanic population and the presence of religious traditions from all over the world have altered the picture.

Perhaps here we should also observe that the United States is involved to a large extent in promoting Protestantism in Latin America–and hence in the breakup of the Catholic Church–through the work of free church formations. It does so out of the conviction that the Catholic Church is incapable of guaranteeing a stable political and economic system, since it is considered an unreliable educator of nations. The underlying expectation is that the free churches model, instead, will be able to create a moral consensus and to form a democratic public will that are similar to those of the United States.

To further complicate the picture, we have to acknowledge that the Catholic Church today represents the largest single religious community in the United States, while American Catholics have incorporated the traditions of the free church regarding the relationship between the Church and politics, believing that a Church that is separate from the state better guarantees the moral foundation of the country. Hence the promotion of the democratic ideal is seen as a moral duty that is in profound compliance with the faith. In this position we can rightly see a continuation, adapted to the times, of the model of Pope Gelasius described earlier.

Let us return to the situation in Europe. In the nineteenth century, the two models that I described above were joined by a third, socialism, which quickly split into two different branches, one totalitarian and the other democratic. Democratic socialism managed to fit within the two existing models as a welcome counterweight to the radical liberal positions, which it developed and corrected. It also managed to appeal to various religious denominations. In England it became the political party of the Catholics, who had never felt at home among either the Protestant conservatives or the liberals. In Wilhelmine Germany, too, Catholic groups felt closer to democratic socialism than to the rigidly Prussian and Protestant conservative forces. In many respects, democratic socialism was and is close to Catholic social doctrine, and has in any case made a remarkable contribution to the formation of a social consciousness.

The totalitarian model, by contrast, was associated with a rigidly materialistic, atheistic philosophy of history: it saw history deterministically, as a road of progress that passes first through a religious and then through a liberal phase to arrive at an absolute, ultimate society in which religion is surpassed as a relic of the past and collective happiness is guaranteed by the workings of material conditions.

This scientific façade hides a dogmatic intolerance that views the spirit as produced by matter, and morals as produced by circumstances. According to its dictates, morals should be defined and practiced on the basis of society's purposes, and everything is deemed moral that helps to usher in the final state of happiness. This dogmatism completely subverts the values that built Europe. It also breaks with the entire moral tradition of humankind by rejecting the existence of values independent of the goals of material progress. Depending on circumstance, anything can become legitimate and even necessary; anything can become moral in the new sense of the term. Even humankind itself can be treated as an instrument, since the individual does not matter, only the future, the cruel deity adjudicating over one and all.

The communist systems collapsed under the weight of their own fallacious economic dogmatism. Commentators have nevertheless ignored all too readily the role in this demise played by the communists' contempt for human rights and their subjugation of morals to the demands of the system and the promises of the future. The greatest catastrophe encountered by such systems was not economic. It was the starvation of souls and the destruction of the moral conscience.

The essential problem of our times, for Europe and for the world, is that although the fallacy of the communist economy has been recognized—so much so that former communists have unhesitatingly become economic liberals—the moral and religious question that it used to address has been almost totally repressed. The unresolved issue of Marxism lives on: the crumbling of man's original uncertainties about God, himself, and the universe. The decline of a moral conscience grounded in absolute values is still our problem today. Left untreated, it could lead to the self-destruction of the European conscience, which we must begin to consider as a real danger—above and beyond the decline predicted by Spengler.[13]

Where Are We Today?

This brings us to the question of how we think things are going today. Amid the major upheavals of the present, is there a European identity that has a future and to which we can be wholeheartedly committed? I am not prepared to enter into a detailed discussion of the European Constitution. I would only like to indicate briefly the basic moral elements that in my opinion should not be missing from that document.

A first element is the unconditionality with which human rights and human dignity should be presented as values that take precedence over the jurisdiction of any state. Fundamental rights are neither created by the lawmaker nor granted to the citizen, "But rather they exist in their own right and must always be respected by lawmakers, to whom they are given beforehand as values belonging to a higher order."[14] The value of human dignity, which takes precedence over all political action and all political decision-making, refers to the Creator: only He can establish values that are grounded in the essence of humankind and that are inviolable. The existence of values that cannot be modified by anyone is the true guarantee of our freedom and of human greatness; in this fact, the Christian faith sees the mystery of the Creator and the condition of man, who was made in God's image.

Today almost no one would openly deny the primacy of human dignity and of basic human rights over any political decision. The horrors of Nazism and its racist doctrine are still too fresh in memory. However, in the concrete sphere of the supposed progress of medicine, there are very real threats to these values. If one considers cloning, the storing of human fetuses for research purposes and for organ harvesting, and the whole field of genetic manipulation, no one can fail to have noticed the threat represented by the slow erosion of human dignity. The situation is only made worse by the increased trafficking in human beings, new forms of slavery, and trafficking in human organs for the sake of transplants. To justify such unjustifiable means, "good ends" are cited repeatedly.

Let us summarize: the values of human dignity, freedom, equality, and solidarity should be inscribed in the European Constitution alongside the fundamental principles of democracy and rule of law. The image of man, the moral option, enshrined in these rights should not be taken for granted. It should instead be recognized as crucial to European identity. The European Constitution must safeguard these values, also in terms of their concrete consequences. However, they can only be defended if there is a corresponding moral conscience that is in a state of constant renewal.

A second element that characterizes European identity is marriage and the family. Monogamous marriage–both as a fundamental structure for the relationship between men and women and as the nucleus for the formation of the state community–was forged already in the Biblical faith. It gave its special character and its special humanity to Europe, both in the West and in the East, precisely because the form of fidelity and sacrifice described here should always be regained through great struggles and suffering.

Europe would no longer be Europe if this fundamental nucleus of its social edifice were to vanish or be changed in an essential way. We all know how much marriage and the family are in jeopardy. Their integrity has been undermined by the easier forms of divorce, at the same time as there has been a spread in the practice of cohabitation between a man and a woman without the legal form of marriage.

Paradoxically, homosexuals are now demanding that their unions be granted a legal form that is more or less equivalent to marriage. Such a development would fall outside the moral history of humanity. Regardless of the diverse legal systems that exist, humankind has never lost sight of the fact that marriage is essentially the special communion of man and woman, which opens itself to children and thus to family.

The question this raises is not of discrimination but of what constitutes the human person as a man or as a woman, and which union should receive a legal form. If the union between man and woman has strayed further and further from legal forms, and if homosexual unions are perceived more and more as enjoying the same standing as marriage, then we are truly facing a dissolution of the image of humankind bearing consequences that can only be extremely grave.

The final element of the European identity is religion. I do not wish to enter into the complex discussion of recent years, but to highlight one issue that is fundamental to all cultures: respect for that which another group holds sacred, especially respect for the sacred in the highest sense, for God, which one can reasonably expect to find even among those who are not willing to believe in God. When this respect is violated in a society, something essential is lost. In our contemporary society, thank goodness, anyone who dishonors the faith of Israel, its image of God, or its great figures must pay a fine. The same holds true for anyone who dishonors the Koran and the convictions of Islam. But when it comes to Jesus Christ and that which is sacred to Christians, instead, freedom of speech becomes the supreme good. The argument has been made that restricting freedom of speech would jeopardize or even abolish tolerance and freedom overall. There is one major restriction on freedom of speech, however: it cannot destroy the honor and the dignity of another person. Lying or denying human rights is not freedom.

This case illustrates a peculiar Western self-hatred that is nothing short of pathological. It is commendable that the West is trying to be more open, to be more understanding of the values of outsiders, but it has lost all capacity for self-love. All that it sees in its own history is the despicable and the destructive; it is no longer able to perceive what is great and pure. What Europe needs is a new self-acceptance, a self-acceptance that is critical and humble, if it truly wishes to survive.

Multiculturalism, which is so constantly and passionately promoted, can sometimes amount to an abandonment and denial, a flight from one's own heritage. However, multiculturalism cannot survive without common foundations, without the sense of direction offered by our own values. It definitely cannot survive without respect for the sacred. Multiculturalism teaches us to approach the sacred things of others with respect, but we can only do this if we, ourselves, are not estranged from the sacred, from God. We can and we must learn from that which is sacred to others. With regard to others, it is our duty to cultivate within ourselves respect for the sacred and to show the face of the revealed God, of the God who has compassion for the poor and the weak, for widows and orphans, for the foreigner; the God who is so human that He Himself became man, a man who suffered, and who by His suffering with us gave dignity and hope to our pain.

Unless we embrace our own heritage of the sacred,

we will not only deny the identity of Europe, we will also fail in providing a service to others to which they are entitled. To the other cultures of the world, there is something deeply alien about the absolute secularism that is developing in the West. They are convinced that a world without God has no future. Multiculturalism itself thus demands that we return once again to ourselves.

We do not know how things will go in Europe in the future. The Charter of Fundamental Rights may be a first step, a sign that Europe is once again consciously seeking its soul. Here we must agree with Toynbee that the fate of a society always depends on its creative minorities. Christian believers should look upon themselves as just such a creative minority, and help Europe to reclaim what is best in its heritage and to thereby place itself at the service of all humankind.

Letter to Joseph Ratzinger

FROM MARCELLO PERA

Your Eminence,

If Europe were to disappear from the face of the Earth, the survivors would probably continue to argue over whether Spengler or Toynbee was right. They might even agree that both were: Spengler, because cultures and civilizations are indeed like organisms, which are subject to the normal, irreversible biological sequence; Toynbee, because you could claim that Europe disappeared through a failure on the part of its creative minorities.

Personally I am more inclined to take Toynbee's view, but I will not belabor the point since I suspect that my skepticism toward Spengler is related to my anguish over his predictions, not unlike the anguish any man feels when he becomes aware of his imminent passing. At the end of the day, we do not know the future and Europe has not vanished. As a group of nations, in fact, it is big, fat, rich, and satisfied. As an international entity, it even emits occasional signs of active political and spiritual life. Our task today, however, is to chart out a course of future action by examining the current state of Europe and its possible and desirable developments. To echo your own words, "Where are we today?" and "How do we want things to be going?"

If we approach the first question from an institutional, political, economic, and social perspective, then there is some consolation to be found in statistical analyses and in the daily experience of the European people, who are becoming more unified and prosperous. If we approach it, instead, from a cultural, moral, and spiritual point of view, we must look beyond the material data, which we can only do if we shift from the first to the second question. Nor could it be otherwise: we can only find out whether we are moving in the right direction if we first understand where we intend to go.

One way to broaden our inquiry is to survey the history of the proposal to insert a specific reference to the Christian or Judaeo-Christian roots of Europe in the preamble to the now defunct European Constitutional Treaty. It became the occasion for a perfunctory debate in the European parliaments and utter silence on the part of European public opinion. In your lecture, you mentioned Europe's "founding moral elements," which I agree should not be absent from a charter that seeks to give Europe an identity and not merely a list of principles, values, and institutions. It is in light of these founding elements that we can assess the present state of Europe and the direction in which it is going.

In discussing your lecture, I wish to raise four questions suggested to me by your bold and perceptive reflections. I have already covered some of this material in my own lecture, but other points are new and fall outside of its purview.

First question: Does the European Constitutional Treaty, the most ambitious charter that Europe has ever signed, provide a satisfactory definition of Europe's identifying, founding elements? I would answer that no, it does not.

Second question: Why did Europe fail in its efforts to draft a true constitution? I would answer that today's Europe lacks the necessary conviction in its own principles and belief in its own values.

Third question: Could the community of European Christians and the Church become more involved in the articulation of such principles? I would answer that yes, they could, because Christians and both the Catholic Church and the national churches have been the historical bearers of the founding principles that European culture and civilization have championed throughout the world; and provided that these principles, along with the churches, are not imprisoned in what you called a "ghetto of subjectivity" in an interview with *Le Figaro* on August 13, 2004.

Fourth question: Since this reference to believers seems to exclude non-believers, what role do they play?

My discussion of the first question is short. The general preamble of the European Constitutional Treaty cites the "cultural, religious, and humanistic inheritance" of Europe. This mention is a little less general than the reference to "spiritual and moral heritage" made in the preamble to the second part (the Charter of Fundamental Rights), but it is still overly vague. To speak of a religious Europe rather than a Christian Europe is analogous to speaking of a human being rather than an Italian citizen: some elements of an identity are conveyed but not enough to make an exact identification. Nor do I believe the argument that this description is clarified when the reader moves from the preamble to the articles of the

Treaty, especially the articles on the rights of European citizens, since if such an argument is true, it necessarily conceals an element of insincerity.

If Europe is Christian by virtue of the values and principles enshrined in the articles of its founding charter, in fact, why then should it be described simply as "religious" in the preamble that summarizes these values and identifies their roots? Or is the adjective "religious" perhaps a substitute for the more generic expression, "spiritual and moral," as written in the preamble to the second part? Can anyone really think that saying Europe is spiritual and moral will give it a distinctive place on a cultural and geopolitical map of the world? My answer is no. The Constitutional Treaty does indeed denote the class of members to whom it refers (European citizens), but it falls far short of connoting a common spirit. The rights guaranteed by the Treaty are a precious heritage, but they are left hanging from a thread since they are proclaimed indistinctly, declaimed as if they were fatherless, created *ex nihilo*.

So why did this happen? This is my second question.

Because Europe is infected by an epidemic of relativism. It believes that all cultures are equivalent. It refuses to judge them, thinking that to accept and defend one's own culture would be an act of hegemony, of intolerance, that betrayed an anti-democratic, anti-liberal, disrespectful attitude toward the autonomy of other populations and individuals. To a Europe that thinks along such lines, the word "spiritual" is palatable because it is so generic, as is the word "religious," because it is vague, obvious, and widely shared. The word "Christian," by contrast, is considered unacceptable, because it is an identifying adjective: appropriate, precise, and therefore suspected of arrogance.

There is no need to mention the debt that Europe owes to Christianity for its birth and its current state. You have covered this in your lecture, and I in mine, as have many others. If Europe today forgets, conceals, or disputes this baptism—which is so manifestly demonstrable—we cannot blame a short memory or short-sightedness, but rather Europe's wish to forget or conceal its Christian roots, and its inability to want things to be otherwise. Your description of the West as having "lost the capacity for self-love" is especially true for Europe. A non-European West does indeed exist—I am thinking in particular of the United States. Despite the allure of the relativists, America still loves itself well, and has indeed been criticized for loving itself too well. European intellectuals and politicians have criticized it as unilateralist, monoculturalist, imperialistic, and bellicose, to name just some of the verbal abuse that has been heaped upon it.

Your analysis is quite striking when you describe the outside impression one gets that "Europe's value system, culture, and faith—in other words, the very foundations of its identity—have reached the end of the road, and have indeed already departed from the scene"; and when you argue that Europe "seems hollow, as if it were internally paralyzed." I do agree that there is a Western self-hatred that is "nothing short of pathological," and that "All that it sees in its own history is the despicable."

The signs of this pathology are everywhere, especially, in my view, in the prison-house of insincerity and hypocrisy known as political correctness. Europe has locked itself in this cage for fear of saying things that are not at all incorrect but rather ordinary truths, and to avoid facing its own responsibilities and the consequences of what might be said. Political correctness does allow itself some liberties. For example, if someone feels like it and truly believes it (perhaps out of poor taste), he is allowed to say that the tuxedo is better than the caftan. However, try saying that the nations of men who wear tuxedos—

after centuries of struggle and untold bloodshed–
have built better states and societies than the men in
caftans. All metaphors aside, try saying that Western
institutions are better than the institutions in Islamic
countries. A warrant will be sworn out for your cultural arrest. You will be banished from the literary sa-
lons, clubs, and academies. You can forget about
winning any book prizes or being invited to speak at
a conference or symposium. The adjective "better" is
forbidden. Even "preferable" is suspect. "Desirable" is
so-so, as long as you are smart enough to use it sub-
jectively, to describe Sacher Torte, for example.
"Equal," instead, is perfect, with its inference that all
societies are equal and some are . . . "more equal than
others."

The prohibition does not go both ways, however
odd that may seem. There are hundreds of examples.
If President George Bush says that there is an axis of
evil, he is decried not for bad policies, but rather as a
cowboy or an illiterate–an accusation one could of
course never make of a European intellectual, ever
wise, profound, and knowledgeable. Noam Chomsky
can claim without qualms that the United States is a
"leading terrorist state." José Saramago can compare
Prime Minister Sharon to Hitler, the Israelis to Nazis,
and even write, "Ah, yes, the horrendous massacres

of civilians caused by the so-called suicide terrorists ... horrendous, yes, doubtless; condemnable, yes, doubtless; but Israel still has a lot to learn if it is not capable of understanding the reasons that can bring a human being to turn himself into a bomb."

But could one likewise criticize another state or even the Palestinian Authority? Not on your life. In your lecture, you offer another example of the lack of reciprocity: "In our contemporary society, thank goodness, anyone who dishonors the faith of Israel ... must pay a fine. The same holds true for anyone who dishonors the Koran. ... But when it comes to Jesus Christ and that which is sacred to Christians, instead, freedom of speech becomes the supreme good." This is curious in a world where all cultures are supposed to be equal.

One symptom of the West's pathology that you indicate–and on which we agree–is the manner in which Europe professes multiculturalism. Europe has become increasingly a magnet for immigration because of its citizens' prosperity and because of its own rights. It has tried to coexist with immigration by slowly transforming itself, without a clear plan, into an American-style melting pot. It has forgotten, however, that every entrant into the American melting pot has to obey the laws of the host country, while the host in his turn respects the visitors, without abdicating his own laws, flag, Constitution, or any other part of itself. The American Constitution is not just an ordinary document drawn up to facilitate the simple coexistence of peoples. In the words of John Adams, one of the founding fathers, the Constitution "was made only for a moral and religious people." Take away religion and you take away the melting pot. Call religion a simple "spiritual inheritance" and the melting pot turns into a vague aggregate without true integration.

For a person to be integrated into society, one must first be clear and firm about what he or she is being integrated into. Integration cannot be accomplished by just saying that our house is so hospitable, so big, so divested of its own symbols (starting with the crucifix), with room enough for the visitor or anyone else to do whatever they may want. Such an attitude, as you say, amounts to "a flight from one's own things." Integration is different, profoundly different, from aggregation. Integration presumes that there is a dialogue that takes the host's position as a starting point. The only thing that aggregation presumes is indulgence. Integration does not mean having equal departure points. It means sharing an equal willingness to accept the common arrival point.

Another syndrome of Western European pathology has appeared more recently. I am referring to war. This is a delicate issue, I know, but one that we must address.

I will not enter into the merits of whether sending troops to fight Saddam Hussein's Iraq was the right thing to do, or was done at the right time or in the right way. I will only speak of war per se, because such a large swathe of European public opinion rejects war per se. Europe, according to Catalan leader Jordi Pujol, is suffering from "angelism." In an article, or rather a manifesto, that appeared simultaneously in the *Frankfurter Allgemeine Zeitung* and *Libération* on May 31, 2003, two European philosophers, Jacques Derrida and Jürgen Habermas, went so far as to proclaim that a new European public opinion was born on February 15, 2003, when the "mass protests in London, Rome, Madrid, Barcelona, Berlin, and Paris reacted to a *coup de main*." The crowds were protesting the document signed by eight European countries disassociating themselves from the two European countries that were opposed to the United States' policy of intervention in Iraq.

To lend substance and a portion of nobility to their argument, the European secular intellectuals took refuge in Kant's "perpetual peace," forgetting that for good old Immanuel, the world government that such a peace could assure was an *idea* and not a *concept*. They were joined in this pacifist conviction by the Church and by Christian culture, especially the clergy.

While angelism certainly has its appeal, realism should not be sacrificed on the altar of its attractiveness, unless one believes, for example, that Auschwitz, the death camps, the second world war, and so many other conflicts and massacres were the results of momentary distraction by God or fortuitous accidents of Kant's pure reason. Evil does indeed exist in the world, and man is no longer an angel because he has eaten from the Tree of Knowledge and lost the earthly paradise. International relations, despite all attempts to civilize, legalize, and democratize them (in other words, to bring them closer to Kant's idea), cannot get rid of force and therefore cannot disregard evil. For populaces, war is a fact of history and coexistence, just as for human beings death is a fact of biology and growth.

Nor can one say that war is immoral, because that would be a *metábasis eis állo génos* (a step to a different category): it would be like saying that death is immoral. What is immoral is immoral war, such as a war to annex a state; or an immoral death, such as a death caused by murder. Facts are facts. It goes without saying that we should do everything possible to avert the fact of war, to prevent it. But to say that we should turn our eyes away when there is a war is not very helpful to the cause of peace. Blessed are those who can prevent a war, not those who repudiate the concept. And blessed are those who when there is a war, are able to fight with a minimum of harm, not those who surrender to the enemy without a struggle.

So why should Europe reject the very fact of war? Why should the same Church that once launched crusades refuse to see that a war has been declared against "Jews and crusaders," as Islamic terrorists say every day? Do the Church and Europe realize that their very existence is at stake, their civilization has been targeted, their culture is under attack? Do they understand that what they are being called on to defend is their own identity? Through culture, education, diplomatic negotiations, political relations, economic exchange, dialogue, preaching, but also, if necessary, through force?

I fear that Europe has not realized this. And thus I fear that European pacifism, however noble and generous it may be, is not so much a realistic, meditated, conscious choice as a heedless, passive consequence of its angelic relativism. This is why I speak of the spirit of Munich, which has an additional irritant today. Namely, that relativism, after teaching that all cultures and all civilizations are equal, makes the contradictory insinuation that our culture and our civilization are worse than others. Hence, there has been a spread–especially throughout Europe–of a sense of guilt, of self-flagellation, of a need for forgiveness from which not even the Church is exempt, together with a feeling of smugness over the dangers avoided. The September 11 atrocity? Blame it on our own genocidal acts, says Chomsky. Suicide bombs? Our fault: We have reduced the Palestinians to desperation, says Saramago. And so on, accompanied by a crescendo of breast-beating. How can we restore realism to a Europe that thinks along such lines?

Which brings me to my third question: Can Christian believers do something to correct the course Europe has taken?

I, too, say yes, and I appreciate the courage of your convictions. I agree that we must commit to defending certain basic values, principles, and institutions, such as human dignity (a Christian concept), heterosexual marriage and the family (a biological and natural concept), and respect for other religions (a cultural concept that gained ground in Europe especially after the religious wars).

All of this is tremendously important, especially today, when some of these values, principles, and institutions are under assault in half of Europe by "secular" legislatures. This is not enough, however. We need to search for a broader and deeper spirit, a general conceptual framework for these values, principles, and institutions, and a common feeling that gives them breathing room, cultural weight, and the force of custom. Morever, then we need to find people who will be the bearer of this spirit.

For this purpose, you appeal—in what I think is both the most courageous and dramatic moment in your lecture—to Toynbee's notion of "creative minorities," and state that "Christian believers should look upon themselves as just such a creative minority." Since Christians in Europe are hardly a minority in a numerical sense, I imagine that you are calling out to the consciously and courageously creative minorities.

Whether they will respond, I do not know, but, I am sure, that they are able to. And it is my firm conviction that this work of renewal should be done by Christians and secularists together. What we need today is a *civil religion* that can instill its values throughout the long chain that goes from the individual to the family, groups, associations, the community, and civil society, *without* passing through the political parties, government programs, and force of states, and therefore without affecting the separation, in the temporal sphere, between church and state. In Europe and in the West so enriched by Europe, such a religion would already be Christian by nature because the Western European tradition is Christian. What I am suggesting is therefore a *non-denominational Christian religion*. As I envision it, this religion would have more monasteries than central churches, more monks that articulate and communicate than church officials, more practitioners than preachers.

In advancing this idea, I am not questioning the liberal principle of separation between church and state. Nor am I questioning the separation between the public and the private spheres. In my opinion, these are achievements of (Western) civilization. I imagine that you agree, judging from the interview you granted to *Le Figaro,* in which you state, "We are in favor of secularism, correctly understood." To allay any suspicions, allow me to note that separation is not the same thing as caesura. Without a civil religion, a society cannot live. A state is never profane: it is always and also paternalistic, and therefore has moral purposes. The modern democratic and social state is especially paternalistic and moral. In its desire to care for its citizens (from cradle, if not sooner, to grave), it must necessarily adopt and safeguard within its own public sphere many values that are widespread in the private sphere of individuals, groups, or categories.

A non-denominational Christian religion is therefore both private and public. Private, because of the faith of the individuals who profess it. Public, because it is the common spirit and feeling of the civil society that it sustains.

Of the models that you mention, I am thinking of free churches and competing churches. This is a difficult model, because it asks the Catholic Church to figure as one of many churches, and to do a two-step: one step backward with respect to the protections accorded to its creed, and one step forward with respect to the militant commitment of its faithful. Free churches along these lines would endow European society with values and give Europe a stronger identity, a deeper sense of its own community. The missionaries of such churches would become more effective preachers.

And finally, what about agnostics or secularists? This last question concerns the family to which I belong. How can secularists participate in the mission of a non-denominational Christian religion?

Of the various differences between secularists and believers, very few of them regard morals. The main difference lies in the *origins* that each group ascribes to their values. For secularists, values come from elsewhere: evolution, education, reason, natural light, social influences, or other factors. For believers values come from Revelation: they are a divine gift, given to us through transcendence. While for secularists values are *constructed* by human effort—through immanence—for believers they are *given* by God.

When it comes to the actual values themselves, however, there are very few differences. For example, secularists place the commandments of Moses in such high esteem that transgression of them is often a punishable offense in state penal codes. The dignity and autonomy of the person, the brotherhood of man, the absence of differences between human beings—three values from the Gospels—were translated into the triad "liberty, fraternity, equality," which, as Pope John Paul II said at Lourdes in August 2004, are also Christian values. The same holds true for mercy, justice, and peace.

There is, however, one important point of difference that is often the source of genuine controversy between secularists and believers: the hierarchy of values. While believers accept the existence of such a hierarchy, secularists do not, claiming that not all values can coexist, and that in some circumstances they can even contradict each other. So while for believers values are ends in themselves that belong to an orderable whole (which is in fact ordered by the Scriptures and by authorized interpretations), for secularists they are instrument-ends that serve other ends, and there is no single end-in-itself capable of ordering all the others. Therefore, for secularists, the instrument-ends are always subordinate to an assessment of their place in the hierarchy. Including life, which for secularists also serves as an instrument-end for the achievement of other ends, and which has value (it is a value) to the extent that it serves these other ends.

These differences over ordinability are most visible in disagreements over bioethical issues. Consider, for example, the case of therapeutic abortion to save the life of a mother (although the same argument can be applied to non-therapeutic abortion). The moral obligation or commandment to respect the human person applies to everybody, secularists and believers alike. For a secularist, however, it is hard to think that this obligation should be interpreted in the sole sense of sacrificing the life of the mother to save that of the newborn. Or consider the case of homologous artificial insemination to treat a sterile couple (although artificial insemination donor procedures also provide an example). Here, too, generating a child, giving life, and loving are values for everybody, but for a secularist it is hard to admit that this value can be fulfilled only by assisting the casual or blind nature of coupling. Secularists must beware—and often they are not wary enough, because technological devices are so readily available—of rushing to transform their whims into desires, and their desires into rights. Believers must also beware—and they, too, are often not wary enough, since it is so easy to find a proper or ad hoc passage from the Scriptures—of transforming their interpretations of the Scriptures into dogma. Both sides must discuss this issue, within their own groups and with each other.

The times in which we live make it hard to enter into such a discussion. Today, as a result of scientific achievements, our values—the values of both secularists and believers—are subject to challenges that would have been unimaginable yesterday. Genetic engineering, genetic manipulation, cloning, and various kinds of biological reproduction raise new problems for which we are so unprepared that sometimes we settle too quickly on solutions, because of philosophical or ethical hubris, petty interests, improvised conventions, or premature action.

One example of such improvisation or prevarication is when one person says that an embryo or a "pre-embryo" is not a person before a given date, as if the predicate "person" were empirical, and could be applied on the basis of its having certain cells, rather than on the basis of what it actually is, namely, a moral and religious concept that cannot be defined in terms of experimental science alone. A similar improvisation is observed in discussions of human cloning. Here I will use the wise, expert words of Italy's Minister of Health, Girolamo Sirchia, in an interview he gave to the newspaper *Libero* on August 14, 2004: "To trivialize the ethical question, the explanation has been offered that, since in cloning they do not use spermatozoa but rather replace the nucleus of a human cell with the nucleus of a somatic cell, then the product on which they are working is not an embryo, and so they can toy with it without moral qualms."

Unlike my secularist brothers and sisters, who thereby sidestep the issue, I have always been of a different persuasion. Since there is no significant gap or qualitative difference between the pre-embryo and the embryo. Since the concept of pre-embryo is a conventional one that refers only to the degree of cellular complexity. Since "personhood" is not an empirical concept (unlike, for example, the concepts of psyche, consciousness, or intelligence), but rather an axiologically loaded one. I have never believed in allowing philosophical questions to be dictated by the contingencies or conveniences of practical decisions, such as experimenting with, correcting, and manipulating embryos. This is why I believe that from a philosophical and moral point of view, we must take the position that an embryo is a person from the moment of conception.

My belief is also grounded in practical considerations. A person is not a thing. Therefore if we recognize the personhood of the embryo from its first moment, we would all become more responsible.

Scientists would become more responsible when they face genetic and biological questions, since they would no longer believe that they were dealing only with questions of fact rather than also with questions of value, or claim that their discoveries in themselves represent progress, as if *bonum et verum et factum convertuntur*–the good, the true, and the made are convertible–always and everywhere.

Lawmakers would become more responsible. When they try to get the green light for this or that congressional bill, they would have to do a better, more accurate job of weighing the ethical reasons on one side of the balance against the practical, scientific, social, and economic issues on the other.

Health workers would also become more responsible. When they act they would be less inclined to experiment, dare, and lightheartedly believe that if something is possible scientifically then it is allowed in practice, so long as you have the instruments and the means.

Finally, the patients of biomedical technologies and all citizens would become more responsible. Everybody would be less propelled to second their desires, transform them into needs, consider them values, and construe them as rights.

More responsible does not mean less free. Recognizing the personhood of the embryo from the moment of birth does not automatically imply taking a single position, such as banning abortion, artificial insemination, or experimentation with embryos. Here the very general reasons I have mentioned on the justification of values hold true. For a secularist even the human person is an instrument-end and as such, subject to an ethical negotiation with other instrument-ends. Since he does not believe in a particular faith, since he does not believe that personhood is a divine gift, since he does not believe that "person" has a single meaning, the secularist, in specific circumstances and for specific reasons, may decide otherwise. For example, in cases of artificial insemination or abortion, the secularist may decide that the personhood of the embryo and the personhood of the fetus can be sacrificed for the sake of the personhood of the mother and the personhood of the pregnant woman. What constitutes prohibition for a believer *might* instead be allowable for a secularist. I say "might" rather than "should," unless the secularists would prefer to be knuckleheads (unfortunately there are many) who speak without thinking and act accordingly.

Even for true secularists these are always tough and often dramatic decisions, because conflicts of values are always tough and often dramatic. To make such decisions, we secularists—at least those of us who wish to be responsible and consciously take our own decisions—have no science available to us. The science of good and evil is something we left behind when we were driven out or went on our way. Our belief in reason helps but it does not exonerate us from risk, from the gamble. Our eyes are still filled with admiration for Plato's science of virtue, Spinoza's *Ethica more geometrico demonstrata* (Ethics demonstrated through the method of geometry),

Leibniz's *Calculemus* (Let us calculate), Kant's categorical imperative, and many other brilliant efforts undertaken by our greatest thinkers to enlighten us. Despite all these intellectual riches, however, we are still searching.

The fact of the matter is, as Bertrand Russell observed in the last century, that there is a dramatic gap between our scientific achievements, which progress rapidly, and our moral standards, which crawl along at a slower pace. Rather than engage in reductionism, and treat ethics as a historical accident–something the relativists would have us do–it would be useful for European culture today to remember, perhaps, one of its founding fathers, Aristotle, who to avoid falling into the relativism of the Sophists on one side, and the dogmatism of Plato on the other, introduced the concept of practical wisdom, *phrónesis,* that is neither a technique of action nor a science of the good, but rather "the true and reasoned state or capacity to act with regard to the things that are good or bad for man."[1]

I repeat, however, that these are tough, unsolved questions that require research, modesty, and openness to mutual understanding. The discussion of the reasons for the differences between secularists and believers must not be paralyzed by a spurious dichotomy between the supposed "secularist values" of the former and the "sacred values" of the latter. And both the tendency toward arrogance of the former and the inclination toward dogmatism of the latter must be rejected.

This is not an easy task, and the road to a civil, non-denominational religion is not easy either. But it is not impossible. I believe that it is our duty to travel it, because the other paths toward giving Europe a self-consciousness have proven to be ephemeral. Absolute profanity, supposing that there is such a thing, is an absolute vacuum in which neither the happy majority nor the creative minorities can exist.

Letter to Marcello Pera

FROM JOSEPH RATZINGER

Mr. President:

First I wish to thank you for your remarkable lecture on relativism, which provides such a precise and thorough analysis of the basic problem of the Western world and its consequences. In this context I would like to leave aside the issue of my possible judgment of President Bush's policies and the war in Iraq, which would require a concrete assessment of the facts and therefore go beyond the scope of the problems that I, as a theologian, can and wish to address publicly. Nor do I wish to dwell on the problem of just war. The *Catechism of the Catholic Church*, backed by the authority of the Church's Magisterium, has already said everything there is to be said about this issue in terms of the Christian faith (numbers 2307–2317, and 2327 ff.). You and I are of a single mind in rejecting a pacifism that does not recognize that some values are worthy of being defended and that assigns the same value to everything. To be in favor of peace on such a basis would signify anarchy, which is blind to the foundations of freedom. Because if everyone is right, no one is right.

This is not a subject on which I wish to write. What regards me directly and demands a response is rather your idea of a non-denominational Christian religion. Once again I must begin with a few words of thanks. It was with great satisfaction that I read your letter of response to my lecture on Europe. I share your diagnosis as well as the orientation of your response. In my capacity as a theologian I feel obliged to clarify the concept of civil religion. I will therefore focus on the relationship between civil religion—which subsumes differences between the single denominations—and faith in the Catholic Church.

Your vision of a Christian civil religion reminds me of Alexis de Tocqueville's work, *Democracy in America*. During his study of the United States, the French scholar had noticed, to put it briefly, that the unstable and fragmentary system of rules on which, to outward appearances, this democracy is founded, functioned because of the thriving Protestant Christian-inspired combination of religious and moral convictions in American society. No one had prescribed or defined these convictions, but everyone assumed them as the obvious spiritual foundation. The recognition of this basic religious and moral orientation, which went beyond the single denominations and defined the society from within, reinforced the corpus of the law. It defined the limits on individual freedoms from within, thereby creating the conditions for a shared, common freedom.

In this regard, I would like to quote a significant phrase from de Tocqueville: "Despotism may govern without faith, but liberty cannot" (Chapter 9). In the letter that you addressed to me, you quote an expression from John Adams that conveys a similar thought, namely, that the American Constitution "was made only for a moral and religious people." In the United States, too, secularization is proceeding at an accelerated pace, and the confluence of many different cultures disrupts the basic Christian consensus. However, there is a much clearer and more implicit sense in America than in Europe that the religious and moral foundation bequeathed by Christianity is greater than that of any single denomination. Europe, unlike America, is on a collision course with its own history. Often it voices an almost visceral denial of any possible public dimension for Christian values.

Why is this so? Why is Europe, which has such an ancient Christian tradition, unable to acknowledge a consensus of this type? A consensus that, irrespective of membership in a specific faith community, accords a sustaining public value to the fundamental concepts of Christianity? Since the historic bases for this difference are well known, I will be brief in my description.

American society was built for the most part by groups that had fled from the system of state churches that reigned in Europe, and they found their religious bearings in free faith communities outside of the state church. The foundations of American society were thus laid by the free churches, which by the tenets of their creed and their very structure are not a state church but rather a free assembly of individuals. In this sense you could say that American society is built on a separation of church and state that is determined and indeed demanded by religion (a separation whose motivation and configuration could not be more different from the conflictual separation of church and state imposed by the French Revolution and the systems that followed it). In America the state is little more than a free space for different religious communities to congregate; it is in its nature to recognize and permit these communities to exist in their particularity and their non-membership in the state. This is a separation that is conceived positively, since it is meant to allow religion to be itself, a religion that respects and protects its own living space distinctly from the state and its ordinances.

This separation has created a special relationship between the state and the private spheres that is completely different from Europe. The private sphere has an absolutely public character. This is why what does not pertain to the state is not excluded in any way, style, or form from the public dimension of social life. Most of America's cultural institutions are non-governmental, such as the universities or arts organizations. The legal and tax system favors and enables this type of non-governmental culture, by contrast to Europe, where, for example, private universities are a recent and only marginal phenomenon. It is safe to say that the free churches also came to see themselves as somewhat relative, but they knew that they were nevertheless united by a common reason above and beyond institutions that was the basis for everything.

This context is not without dangers of its own. Some publications today seem to be reviving the WASP ideology, which holds that the true American is white, of Anglo-Saxon origin, and Protestant. This ideology was born when the arrival of immigrant groups of Catholic faith–especially the Irish, Italians, Poles, and people of color–was perceived as a threat to the consolidated identity of America. These ideas held sway until the twentieth century, in the sense that anyone who aspired to an important position in American public life had to be a WASP. In reality, however, the Catholic community was soon well integrated into the American identity.

American Catholics also recognized the positive character of the separation between church and state, for both religious reasons and for the religious freedom that it guaranteed them. It is also thanks to the significant contribution of Catholics that American society has maintained a Christian consciousness. Their contribution is more important than ever at a time of profound, radical transformations in the Protestant world. Since the traditional Protestant communities are continuously adapting to secularized society, they are losing their internal cohesion and their ability to persuade. The evangelicals, who used to be the most relentless enemies of Catholicism, are not only gaining ground on the traditional communities, but they are also discovering a new commonality with Catholicism. They have come to see Catholicism as a defender against the pressures of secularization and an upholder of the same ethical values that they themselves profess: values that they feel have been betrayed by their Protestant brothers.

On the basis of the structure of Christianity in the United States, the American Catholic bishops made a unique contribution to the Second Vatican Council through their instrumental role in drafting the Declaration *Dignitatis Humanae* on Religious Freedom (1965). They brought to the issue and to the Catholic tradition the experience of the non-state church (which had proven to be a condition for protecting the public value of fundamental Christian principles) as a Christian form that emerged from the very nature of the Church. Today American society–because of massive immigration from Latin America and the growing pressures of secularization–is forced to address serious new challenges. One could say, however–at least in my opinion–that in the United States there is still a civil Christian religion, although it is besieged and its contents have become uncertain.

Why does all of this matter so little to Europe? Why, in Catholic countries, is there such sharp opposition between Catholics and secularists? Why in the varied panorama of secularism is there a prominent fringe that resolutely denies the right of a public presence to the Christian faith and its values? Here, too, the only answer we can derive is from the pages of history.

Ever since the Reformation, Europe has been divided into two spiritual camps: the Catholic part of the continent, which corresponds largely but not wholly to the Latin countries, as well as the nations that formerly belonged to the Hapsburg Empire and Poland and Lithuania; and Protestant Europe, which instead coincides mainly, but not wholly, with the nations of Germanic origin. The Reformed churches were established in Europe as state churches, in part because, for example in England and Scandinavia, the Reformation was introduced by monarchs, and in part because the princes–for example in Germany–anointed themselves as managers, guarantors, and beneficiaries of the Reformation. As we saw, the state church principle later provoked the counter-offensive of the free churches that gave rise to the United States.

The Catholic principle is in contrast with the state church system because it emphasizes the universal nature of the Church, a Church that does not coincide with any one nation or any one state community. This Church lives in all nations. It creates a community–above and beyond loyalty to one's own country–that spreads beyond national borders. Take the example of the Gregorian reform. After many efforts, the Church succeeded in obtaining the distinction between *sacerdotium* and *imperium,* thereby creating the basis for a separation between the two spheres. In fact, from the start of the modern era, European Catholicism was also able to assert a state church system that made the faith, in practice, an affair of state.

The Enlightenment, however, was received in two completely different ways by Protestantism and Catholicism, precisely because of the particular nature of each. While the Enlightenment proclaimed the autonomy of reason and its emancipation from traditional faith, the Catholic Church remained strongly attached to its heritage of faith, thereby locking the two in endless conflict. Despite the many upheavals of the sixteenth century, the Catholic countries did not experience any major religious schisms until the eighteenth century, when the new "denomination" of *laici* (secular people) was born.[1] Since then, the separation between Catholics and *laici* has become characteristic of the Latin countries, while the German-speaking Protestant countries have no such usage as the word *laico,* a term that it finds completely incomprehensible. In the broadest sense of the word, the term *laico* denotes spiritual membership in the Enlightenment. In the two centuries that have gone by since then, no bridge has been built between the Protestant and the Catholic faiths; the two worlds seem to have become mutually impenetrable.

Since "secularity" also means free thinking and freedom from religious constrictions, it also involves the exclusion of Christian contents and values from public life. This exclusion leads to the tendency on the part of the modern conscience to treat the entire realm of faith and morals as "subjective." Thank goodness that the demarcation lines have subsequently been softened and the secular panorama become more varied. On the Catholic side, Vatican II incorporated the collective efforts of theologians and philosophers from the previous two hundred years to open the gates that had divided the faith from the learning of the Enlightenment and embark on a fertile exchange between the two. Thus, while the split between Catholics and secular people would seem to exclude a form of civil religion, openings have appeared that people have wisely utilized.

Before continuing along these lines, we should also examine the European Protestant world and its relationship to secularism.

From the beginning Protestantism has seen itself as a movement of emancipation, liberation, and purification. When I went to Geneva for the first time, everywhere I looked I saw inscriptions such as *Post tenebras lux,* illustrating the close relationship between the Reformation and the basic tendencies of the Enlightenment. In this sense, despite a certain dogmatism that quickly emerged in the Protestant churches, one can still speak of a kinship between the Enlightenment and Protestantism–which became very clear in the eighteenth century. This relationship combined an intensification of the genuinely confessional nature with a broader intertwining of Protestantism and Enlightenment thought.

Friedrich Schleiermacher, who established a new approach to theology at the turn of the nineteenth century, expelled religion from the sphere of reason and gave it what he believed to be a new and secure position within the realm of the sentiments. In this way religion could supposedly survive, although its confessional contents had been reduced mostly to the symbolic sphere.

In the nineteenth century, there were strong reactionary movements that gave new life to the various creeds, although there continued to be a widespread identification of the dominant spiritual movements with the Protestant conscience. In this sense German Protestantism, for one, was broadly transformed into a *religio civilis* in the nineteenth and early twentieth centuries. After the first world war, however, this civil religion appeared to be compromised by its profound commingling with the Prussian national conscience. In the period between the two world wars, there was consequently a major "reconfessionalization" of German Protestantism as well as a new openness toward ecumenism and the Catholic Church.

Today's panorama is quite varied. To do it justice we would have to go well beyond the scope of this short statement. Despite the apparent diversity of the phenomena of state churches, evangelical movements, secularization, and the search for a renewal of the faith, Protestantism as a whole seems to be characterized by a consciousness of its profound intertwining with modern culture. This is both its strength and its weakness, since the fatal tendency to conform to the times–which led Protestantism to the brink of dissolution during the Enlightenment–is alive and well today, as the traditional Protestant churches in the United States demonstrate. Protestantism has thus become, for the most part, a cultural fact: it is somehow still called Protestant, although it is no longer connected to any particular denomination.

In this regard, the words of the former Prime Minister of France, Lionel Jospin, are telling. He called himself an atheistic Protestant. He characterized his atheism in terms of his Protestant cultural origins. I say this because Protestantism—given its openness toward the modern culture, which it helped to mold to a remarkable extent—could appear to be the ideal representative of a civil religion. Yet its current crisis and the deep transformations it has undergone demonstrate that "de-confessionalization" does not automatically produce something that resembles a broad Christianity encompassing other denominations.

Today, in the old confessional churches of Protestantism, there is a steady, disconcerting loss of vitality. Free churches of an evangelical model are being formed that their enemies call "fundamentalist," but that are nonetheless able to attract thousands of people in search of a solid foundation for their lives. Statistics tell us that the more churches adapt themselves to the standards of secularization, the more followers they lose. They become attractive, instead, when they indicate a solid point of reference and a clear orientation. An ambiguous light is thus cast upon the concept of civil religion: if it is no more than a reflection of the majority's convictions, then it means little or nothing. If instead it is a source of spiritual strength, then we have to ask what feeds this source.

So how can Europe attain a Christian civil religion that overcomes the boundaries between denominations and gives voice to values that sustain society rather than console the individual? Such a religion can obviously not be built by experts, since no committee or council, whoever its members, can possibly generate a global ethos. Something living cannot be born except from another living thing. Here is where I see the importance of creative minorities. From a numerical point of view, Christians are still clearly the majority in much of Europe, although the number of the baptized has gone down in some countries, especially in Eastern Europe and northern Germany. In the part of Germany that was formerly under Communist rule, for example, baptized Christians are no longer the majority. Even the existing majorities, however, have grown weary and disenchanted.

This is why it is so important to have convinced minorities in the Church, for the Church, and above all beyond the Church and for society: human beings who in their encounters with Christ have discovered the precious pearl that gives value to all life

(Matthew 13:45 ff.), assuring that the Christian imperatives are no longer ballast that immobilizes humanity, but rather wings that carry it upward. Such minorities are formed when a convincing model of life also becomes an opening toward a knowledge that cannot emerge amid the dreariness of everyday life. Such a life choice, over time, affirms its rationale to a growing extent, opening and healing a reason that has become lazy and tired. There is nothing sectarian about such creative minorities. Through their persuasive capacity and their joy, they reach other people and offer them a different way of seeing things.

Therefore my first thesis is that a civil religion that truly has the moral force to sustain all people presupposes the existence of convinced minorities that have "discovered the pearl" and live it in a manner that is also convincing to others. Without such motivating forces, nothing can be built.

My second thesis is that we all need forms of belonging or of reference to these communities, or simply of contact with them. They are created automatically when their persuasive ability is sufficiently great. The Lord compared the Kingdom of God to a tree on whose branches various birds make their nests (Matthew 13:32). Perhaps the Church has forgotten that the tree of the Kingdom of God reaches beyond the branches of the visible Church, but that this is precisely why it must be a hospitable place in whose branches many guests find solace.

In the times of Jesus, the Jewish diaspora was filled with "God-fearers" who reported in varying degrees to the synagogue and who, in different ways, lived the spiritual treasure of the faith of Israel. Only a few of them wished to enter fully into the community of Israel, through circumcision, but for them it was a reference point that indicated the way to life. Primitive Christianity arose in this environment, giving vital new energy to a dying antiquity. The medieval monastic communities knew forms of belonging or of reference to the monastic family that enabled their energies to renew the Church and society as a whole. Meeting places that become "yeast" (Matthew 13:33)—a persuasive force that acts beyond the more closed sphere until it reaches everybody—should therefore be formed around the minorities that have been touched by faith.

As a third thesis, I would say that these creative minorities can clearly neither stand nor live on their own. They live naturally from the fact that the Church as a whole remains and that it lives in and stands by the faith in its divine origins. It did not invent these origins but it recognizes them as a gift that it is duty-bound to transmit. The minorities renew the vitality of this great community at the same time as they draw on its hidden life force, which forever generates new life.

As the fourth thesis, I would say that both secular people and Catholics, seekers and believers, in the dense thicket of branches filled with many birds, must move toward each other with a new openness. Believers must never stop seeking, while seekers are touched by the truth and thus cannot be classified as people without faith and Christian-inspired moral principles. There are ways of partaking of the truth by which seekers and believers give to and learn from each other. This is why the distinction between Catholics and secularists is relative. Secular people are not a rigid block. They do not constitute a set denomination, or worse, an "anti-denomination." They are people who do not yet feel able to take the step of ecclesiastical faith with everything that such a step involves. Very often they are people who passionately seek the truth, who are pained by the lack of truth in humankind. Consequently they return to the essential contents of culture and faith, and through their commitment often make these contents even more luminous than an unquestioned faith, accepted more out of habit than out of the sufferings of the conscience.

There can be a positive meaning to these various degrees of belonging. Between the internal and the external, as I have already said, there is a mutual giving and receiving. In the 1950s, Hans Urs von Balthasar spoke of "breaking down the barriers," by which he meant this new mutual openness. By going beyond borders, beyond rigid classifications, one could, God willing, form a Christian civil religion that would not be an artificial construction of something that everybody supposedly finds reasonable, but rather a living partaking of the great spiritual tradition of Christianity, in which these values are actualized and revitalized.

To these general reflections on the question of a non-denominational Christian religion, allow me, Mr. President, to add three further observations to complete and expand my previous remarks.

The question of why the Christian faith today is struggling to convey its great message to people in Europe inevitably regards the believing Christian and, above all, the pastor of the Church. I see two main reasons for its difficulties:

a) The first reason was articulated by Nietzsche when he wrote, "Christianity has thus far always been attacked in the wrong way. As long as one does not perceive Christian morality as a capital crime against life, its defenders will always have an easy game. The question of the *truth* of Christianity ... is something entirely secondary as long as the question of the value of Christian morality is not addressed."

Here what we are actually addressing, in my opinion, is the decisive reason for the abandonment of Christianity: its model for life is apparently unconvincing. It seems to place too many restraints on humankind that stifle its *joie de vivre,* that limit its precious freedom, and that do not lead it to open pastures—in the language of the Psalms—but rather into want, into deprivation. Something similar happened in antiquity, when the representatives of the powerful Roman state appealed to Christians by saying: Return to our religion, our religion is joyous, we have feasts, drunken revels, and entertainments, while you believe in One who was crucified.

The Christians were able to demonstrate persuasively how empty and base were the entertainments of paganism, and how sublime the gift of faith in the God who suffers with us and leads us to the road of true greatness. Today it is a matter of the greatest urgency to show a Christian model of life that offers a livable alternative to the increasingly vacuous entertainments of leisure-time society, a society forced to make increasing recourse to drugs because it is sated by the usual shabby pleasures. Living on the great values of the Christian tradition is naturally much harder than a life rendered dull by the increasingly costly habits of our time. The Christian model of life must be manifested as a life in all its fullness and freedom, a life that does not experience the bonds of love as dependence and limitation but rather as an opening to the greatness of life. Here, too, I refer to the idea of the creative minorities that enrich this model of life, present it in a convincing way, and can thus instill the courage needed to live it.

b) The second reason for the crumbling of Christianity lies, in my opinion, in the fact that it seems to have been surpassed by "science" and to be out-of-step with the rationalism of the modern era. This is especially true from two perspectives. Historical criticism has distorted the Bible, undermining the credibility of its divine origin. Science and the modern image of the world it has created seem to exclude from reality the basic vision of the Christian faith, relegating it to the realm of myth. So how can people still be Christians?

The Church and its theology have wasted too much time on small back-guard skirmishes, getting lost in debates over details, and they have not invested enough effort in asking the basic questions: What is Revelation? How does Revelation coming from God link with the development of human history? On the long road of history, so littered with troubles, how is the guidance of the Other manifested—the Other who acts on and renews history in a way beyond the capability of human action?

To engage scientists and engage in dialogue with philosophers of the modern era, we must return to the basic question of what makes the world cohere. Does matter create reason? Does pure chance produce meaning? Or do the intellect, logos, and reason come first, so that reason, freedom, and the good are already part of the principles that construct reality? A valid civil religion will not conceive of God as a mythical entity but rather as a possibility of reason—just as Reason itself precedes and enables our reason to seek to recognize it. I believe that the struggle to regain an image of the world based on spirit and sense, and to counter the deconstructionist trends that you outlined in your lecture, is a great challenge shared by Catholics and secular people alike.

I would now like to say a few words about relativism. As I said at the outset, I am most grateful for all that you explained so carefully in your lecture, and I agree with you completely on everything.

In recent years I find myself noting how the more relativism becomes the generally accepted way of thinking, the more it tends toward intolerance, thereby becoming a new dogmatism. Political correctness, whose constant pressures you have illuminated, seeks to establish the domain of a single way of thinking and speaking. Its relativism creates the illusion that it has reached greater heights than the loftiest philosophical achievements of the past. It prescribes itself as the only way to think and speak–if, that is, one wishes to stay in fashion. Being faithful to traditional values and to the knowledge that upholds them is labeled intolerance, and relativism becomes the required norm. I think it is vital that we oppose this imposition of a new pseudo-enlightenment, which threatens freedom of thought as well as freedom of religion. In Sweden, a preacher who had presented the Biblical teachings on the question of homosexuality received a prison sentence. This is just one sign of the gains that have been made by relativism as a kind of new "denomination" that places restrictions on religious convictions and seeks to subordinate all religions to the super-dogma of relativism.

Finally I wish to add a few words about differences over bioethical issues, which you address in the last pages of your letter. These issues are so complicated that they can only be addressed through an in-depth treatment that is not possible in the form of a letter. I will thus limit myself to a few brief remarks.

I appreciate that you—unlike many other secular people—speak of the "person from the moment of conception," and that you underline the deep ethical difference between the relationship with persons and the relationship with things. I can well understand your observations on therapeutic abortion and on homologous artificial insemination.

The Church's Magisterium deals with the question of how far the Church should go in pressing its demands on lawmakers. The Congregation for the Doctrine of the Faith prepared a document on the responsibilities of Catholic politicians that makes a clear distinction between the two levels at stake. The Catholic will not and should not, through the making of laws, impose a hierarchy of values that can only be recognized and enacted within the faith. He or she can only reclaim that which belongs to the human foundations accessible to reason and therefore essential to the construction of a sound legal order. Yet at this point a spontaneous question arises:

What is this moral minimum accessible to reason that all human beings share? Is it that which all human beings understand? Is it possible to conduct a statistical analysis of these rational common bases for an authentic legal code?

Here the dilemma of human life emerges fully. If we had to place on the same level rationality and the average conscience, very little "reason" would be left in the end. The Christian is convinced that his or her faith opens up new dimensions of understanding, and above all that it helps reason to be itself. There is the true heritage of the faith (the Trinity, the divinity of Christ, the sacraments, and so on), but there is also the knowledge for which faith provides evidence, knowledge that is later recognized as rational and pertaining to reason as such, and thus also implying a responsibility toward others. The person of faith, who has received help in reason, must work in favor of reason and of that which is rational: this, in the face of dormant or diseased reason, is a duty he or she must perform toward the entire human community.

Naturally the person of faith knows that he or she must respect the freedom of others and that ultimately the only weapon is the soundness of the arguments set forth in the political arena and in the struggle to shape public opinion. This is why it is so crucial to develop a philosophical ethics that, while being in harmony with the ethic of faith, must however have its own space and its own logical rigor. The rationality of the arguments should close the gap between secular ethics and religious ethics and found an ethics of reason that goes beyond such distinctions.

Having said this, I wish to address briefly two questions of content. The first problem is that of being a "person from the moment of conception." The Instruction *Donum vitae* of February 22, 1987, under Part I, article 1, recalls how, according to the knowledge of modern genetics, "From the first instant, the program is fixed as to what this living being will be: a man, this individual-man with his characteristic aspects already well determined." In other words, "In the zygote resulting from fertilization the biological identity of a new human individual is already constituted."

Here we shift from the empirical to the philosophical. The Instruction affirms that no experimental datum will ever be sufficient proof of the existence of a spiritual soul. The document formulates the connection between the empirical and philosophical levels in the form of a question. It recalls yet again that one can verify empirically that there is a new individual: "Individual" is an empirical term since it refers to an organism that, while being completely dependent on the mother, is nevertheless a new organism with its own genetic program. Hence the question, "How can a human individual not be a human person?" From this derives the ethical deduction, "The human being must be respected—as a person—from the very first instant of his existence."

Here the Church's Magisterium is not proposing its own philosophical theology, nor is it making a theological argument; it is posing a question at the meeting point of the empirical and philosophical (anthropological) levels that, in my opinion, has clear ethical consequences for reason. From this derives, on the other hand, a deduction for the legislator: if this is the way things are, then the authorization to kill the embryo means that "The state is denying the equality of all before the law" (Part III). For us the question of the right of life for all those who are human beings is not a question of the ethics of faith, but rather of the ethics of reason. It is at this level that the debate should take place.

To address the issues raised by artificial fertility I would need far more space. I would, however, like to at least mention the fact that *Donum vitae*, while rejecting artificial insemination, both homologous and by donor–on the basis of an ethics that is argued anthropologically–does not demand from lawmakers a ban on extra-corporeal homologous artificial insemination, but would prefer to see a legal prohibition on donor artificial insemination, in order to protect the legally sanctioned value of marriage. Not to do so, in other words, would amount to rejecting a fundamental institution of societies based on Christian culture. Such an affront to the foundations of our social structure is essentially a self-contradiction by the lawmaker. The fact that it is no longer perceived as such demonstrates clearly how far the process of dismantling the institution of marriage has progressed. On the basis of my faith and my moral reason, I see here a very serious signal of alarm for our societies.

The last remaining question is whether it is politically realistic to argue with a reason oriented toward faith in creation, an argument that struggles to be understood by the average person today. The Church's most recent documents are fully cognizant of this context. Their starting point is that in the conscience's search for the truth, acceptance and success cannot be decisive criteria. However, they also realize that in politics it is a question of what is feasible and of getting as close as possible to that which the conscience and reason have recognized as the true good for the individual and society. Politics is the art of the compromise. How far can the Christian politician push, through compromises, in favor of a law that is morally grounded without entering into contradiction with his or her conscience?

Article 73 of the encyclical *Evangelium vitae* (1995) drafts a first basic rule whose purport and limits still need to be defined in the theological discussion. Both *Evangelium vitae* and *Donum vitae* acknowledge that, on the basis of reasons subject to disagreement today, the necessary consensus does not exist to pass laws on ethics of life questions that fully correspond to the Christian conscience. Both theses therefore insist that the legislator, on the basis of and within the realm of the principle commonly recognized as freedom of conscience, should concede the right to conscientious objection. The Church does not wish to impose on others that which they do not understand, but it expects that others will at least respect the consciences of those who allow their reason to be guided by the Christian faith.

Where space is not granted to this freedom, the Christian should—according to the *Donum vitae*—claim the right to passive resistance and thereby offer a testimony of conscience that could somehow make people reflect and lead to the formation of a new conscience. This road will become less necessary the more we succeed in developing a civil Christian religion that can shape our conscience as Europeans and—bridging the separation between secularists and Catholics—manifest the reasonable and binding value of the great principles that have edified Europe and can and must rebuild it.

Notes

NOTES TO
Relativism, Christianity, and the West

1. Max Weber, *The Protestant Ethic and the Spirit of Capitalism,* 2d ed., trans. Anthony Giddens. New York: Routledge Classics, 2001. First edition 1992; first English edition 1930.

2. Samuel P. Huntington, *The Clash of Civilizations and the Remaking of the World Order.* New York: Simon and Schuster, 1998. 310.

3. To whoever might take issue with my use of the word "ultimate," I would point out that we reject Nazism, fascism, communism, racism, anti-Semitism, and fanaticism not because they conflict with some logical theorem, or because they are empirically or scientifically false, but because they offend our consciences, contradict our deep intuitions about human

rights, and violate our fundamental values. We reject them, in other words, for practical rather than theoretical reasons.

4. Olivier Roy, *The Failure of Political Islam,* trans. Carol Volk. Cambridge: Harvard University Press, 1996. 9.

5. Ibid., 11.

6. Gilles Kepel is perhaps the most optimistic of these thinkers, but he is equally radical in his analysis: "The uncertainties over the modes of transition from the Islamist era to 'post-Islamism' are reminiscent of the debates on post-communism in former Soviet societies. In both cases, regardless of the solutions found, the situation today documents the ethical failure of a model associated with a period that is historically dated, surpassed and rejected, and no longer with a utopia that was considered the bearer of the future. This defeat goes beyond the borders of Iran and of the Sciite world, and strikes the Islamist ideology as a whole, even in the Sunni world." *Jihad: The Trail of Political Islam,* trans. Anthony F. Roberts. Cambridge, Mass.: Belknap Press, 2003. 415.

7. This type of error–the passage from the descriptive to the prescriptive–is made by several critiques of Huntington's well-known book, which does not *preach* but rather *predicts* future clashes among civi-

lizations. John L. Esposito, for example, after citing Huntington's thesis that a central point of conflict in the immediate future will be between the West and the many Islamic-Confucian states, comments, "This view risks slipping into the racist perception of a cultural threat." *The Islamic Threat: Myth or Reality.* Oxford: Oxford University Press, 1999. 226.

8. Translator's note: The term *pensiero debole,* or "weak thought," was coined in the early 1990s by the Italian philosopher Gianni Vattimo to denote his own brand of nihilism, and has subsequently become a blanket term to describe Italian post-modern thinking.

9. While Wittgenstein was definitely one of the founders of relativism, my reference to his work is not meant to be a claim that he was the first. In philosophy, priorities are always a slippery matter. One could just as easily cite the "linguistic turn," contemporaneous to the analytic philosophy of language, espoused by the hermeneutics of Gadamer ("The being that can be understood is language," Hans-Georg Gadamer, *Truth and Method,* 2d rev. ed., trans. Joel Weinsheimer and Donald G. Marshall. New York: Continuum, 1993. 542); or the ontology of Heidegger ("language is the house of Being," Martin Heidegger, "Letter on Humanism," in *Basic Writings,* ed. David Farrell Krell. New York: Harper and Row,

1977. 217); as well as combinations of the two in thinkers such as Richard Rorty.

10. The technique of *elenchos,* frequently used in both common and specialized argumentation, consists in trying to confute an interlocutor who, for example, may have argued thesis T, proving that from T derives consequence C, and that since C is not true, or C has already been disproved by the interlocutor himself, or even since T was directly or indirectly disproved by another thesis, T^1, which is accepted by the interlocutor. In each case, a rule of elementary logic is applied according to which if a thesis p implies a consequence q, and q proves to be false, then p is also false.

11. Jacques Derrida, *Of Hospitality: Anne Dufourmantelle Invites Jacques Derrida to Respond,* trans. Rachel Bowlby. Cultural Memory in the Present. Stanford, Calif.: Stanford University Press, 2000.

12. Jacques Derrida, *Rogues: Two Essays on Reason,* trans. Pascale-Anne Brault and Michael Naas. Stanford, Calif.: Stanford University Press, 2005. 60.

13. Ibid., 58.

14. Giovanna Borradori, *Philosophy in a Time of Terror: Dialogues with Jürgen Habermas and Jacques Derrida.* Chicago: University of Chicago Press, 2003. 88, 114–15.

15. Ibid., 115.

16. Paul Feyerabend, *Against Method*, 3d ed. New York: Verso, 1993; Thomas S. Kuhn, *The Structure of Scientific Revolutions*, 2d ed., with postscript. Chicago: University of Chicago Press, 1970.

17. Quoted in Arthur C. Danto, *Nietzsche as Philosopher*. New York: Columbia University Press, 2005. 76; Jacques Derrida, *Of Grammatology*, trans. Gayatri Chakravorty Spivak. Baltimore: Johns Hopkins University Press, 1976. 163.

18. Joseph Cardinal Ratzinger, *Truth and Tolerance: Christian Belief and World Religions*, trans. Henry Taylor. Fort Collins, Colo.: Ignatius Press, 2004. 84, 72. Cardinal Ratzinger expressed himself in a similar manner in a speech to the Commission of the Bishops' Conferences in Guadalajara, Mexico, in May 1996: "Relativism has become, in effect, the fundamental problem of faith in our day." *Osservatore Romano*, November 1, 1996. [Translator's note: This speech constitutes the first chapter of the second part of *Truth and Tolerance*.]

19. Ibid., 175.

20. Paul Knitter, *No Other Name?: A Critical Survey of Christian Attitudes toward the World Religions*. Maryknoll, New York: Orbis, 1985. 17.

21. Ibid., 185.

22. Ratzinger, *Truth and Tolerance,* 120.

23. Ibid., 117. While Huntington does not go this far, he does propose a symmetrical thesis: "Imperialism is the necessary logical consequence of universalism." Huntington, *Clash,* 310.

24. Angelo Cardinal Scola, "Cristianesimo e religioni nel futuro dell'Europa," *L'identitá dell'Europa e le sue radici,* Edizioni del Senato. Soveria Mannelli, Italy: Rubbettino, 2002. 39.

25. Among the tasks that the encyclical *Fides et Ratio* (1998) assigns to the Church in the service of humanity, "One way in particular imposes a responsibility of a quite special kind: the *diakonia of the truth.*" Article 2. In this regard, see the comment of Monsignor Rino Fisichella in *Fides et Ratio: I rapporti fra fede e ragione.* Casale Monferrato, Italy: Edizioni Piemme, 1998.

26. This is the approach taken by the "various liberation theologies," to use the expression of a theologian who identifies with them, Juan José Tamayo-Acosta. One of his books contains a long, varied list of assorted African, Asian, Latin American, feminist, ecological, and campesino theologies, all of which share a "no global" perspective since "Their starting point is the great fact of denial of human dignity and marginalization to which nations, peoples, commu-

nities, and social groups are subjected for reasons of gender, race, ethnicity, culture, class, and religion. We are dealing with entire continents excluded because of the hurricane of neo-liberal globalization." Juan José Tamayo-Acosta, "Dignity and Liberation: A Theological and Political Perspective." *Concilium* 2, 2003, 67–77. Apart from this catastrophic viewpoint, one might wonder, at the strictly theological level, whether the reduction of the Christian message to such political and secular values is compatible with its being a religion that places salvation not in this world but in the *otherworldly*, and not for this or that individual, but for *everyone*.

The liberation theologies have recently had to address pluralistic, relativistic strains at the Fourth Parliament of the World's Religions. According to one press report, at the symposium on "Towards an Interreligious and Intercultural Theology of Liberation," in which Knitter and Tamayo-Acosta participated, there was a convergence of views on various issues, including the point that "The religions must acknowledge that violence, poverty, religious intolerance, disease, globalization to the profit of the few, and the mistreatment of the Earth constitute a challenge to which they can and must provide an urgent response." Luigi De Paoli, "A Barcellona il parlamento delle religioni," July 20, 2004, http://ww2.carta.org/articoli/articles/art_678.html. Clearly, the point is that the lowest common denominator among various religions is not religious but secular.

27. John Paul II, Apostolic Exhortation *Ad gentes* (1965), article 9.

28. R. Scott Appleby, "Job Description for the Next Pope." *Foreign Policy,* January-February 2004. 28–34, 31.

29. Piero Gheddo, "Islam, accordo impossibile." *Global Foreign Policy,* March/April 2004. 38, 40.

30. Ibid.

31. These "references" and "corrections" would make an interesting history. At Vatican II, in the declaration *Nostra aetate* (1965), the thesis was approved according to which the different religions "often reflect a ray of that Truth which enlightens all men" (article 2). While it recalls the principle that Christ is "the way, the truth, and the life," the declaration did not say that He is the *only* way. The orientation was instead toward the "universal brotherhood" that seemed to allude to parallel roads to salvation. The fathers of the council and post-conciliar theologians were thus running the risk of relativism.

Twenty-five years later, this risk became a real danger when relativism had gained ground. It is no accident that the title of Chapter 1 of the encyclical *Redemptoris missio* (1990) is "Jesus Christ the *only* Savior," and that it warns against "widespread indifferentism, which, sad to say, is found also among Christians. It is based on incorrect theological perspectives and is characterized by a religious relativism which leads to the belief that 'one religion is as good as another'" (article 36).

The declaration *Dominus Iesus* (2000) makes an even more explicit correction: "The theory of the limited, incomplete, or imperfect character of the revelation of Jesus Christ, which would be complementary to that found in other religions, is contrary to the Church's faith" (article 6). The theory of "Jesus of Nazareth that considers him a particular, finite, historical figure, who reveals the divine not in an exclusive way, but in a way complementary with other revelatory and salvific figures . . . [is] in profound conflict with the Christian faith" (articles 9–10). "It is likewise contrary to the Catholic faith to introduce a separation between the salvific action of the Word as such and that of the Word made man. With the incarnation, all the salvific actions of the Word of God are always done in unity with the human nature that he has assumed for the salvation of all people" (article 10).

32. In the European Constitutional Treaty, the preamble to Part II (the Charter of Fundamental Rights, also known as the "Nice Treaty") mentions the "spiritual and moral heritage" of Europe, while the general preamble takes a step forward in recalling its "cultural, religious, and humanistic inheritance."

33. *Ecclesia in Europa* (June 28, 2003), n. 24. Libreria Editrice Vaticana.

34. The liberals and secularists who feel dismayed today by having to defend Christianity should return to the roots of their doctrine. They would receive great comfort from reading John Locke, for one.

Locke was one of the greatest theorists of liberalism, individualism, the bourgeois spirit, and the notion of "civil society": of free men who respect each other, defend themselves through the rule of law from the sovereign's powers, and practice religious tolerance in opposition to the political will. But when the question is raised of how to give this doctrine foundations and strength, and how to establish a free society, his response was, through Christianity. He writes, for example, "Let it be granted (though not true) that all the moral precepts of the gospel were known by some body or other, amongst mankind, before. . . . What will all this do, to give the world a complete morality, that may be to mankind, the unquestionable rule of life and manners? . . . 'Tis not enough, that there were up and down scattered sayings of wise men, conformable to right reason. . . . But these incoherent apophthegms of philosophers, and wise men, however excellent in themselves and well intended by them, could never make a morality, whereof the world could be convinced; could never rise to the force of a law that mankind could with certainty depend on. . . . 'Tis not every writer of morals, or compiler of it from others, that can thereby be erected into a law-giver to mankind; and a dictator of rules, which are therefore valid, because they are to be found in his books, under the authority of this or that philosopher. . . . Nobody that I know, before Our Saviour's time, ever did, or went about to give us a morality." John Locke, *The Reasonableness of Christianity and a Discourse of Miracles*. Stanford, Calif.: Stanford University Press, 1958. 62–63.

35. Not even the authors of the Enlightenment, so maligned today by post-modern philosophers, failed to recognize the role of Christianity. "Of all the religions that describe themselves as revealed, and thus as the only one that can be embraced, . . . the Christian religion is the best of all religions for States that have the good fortune to have it associated with its political government. . . . While this religion may

seem to have as its sole purpose the happiness of the afterlife, of all religions it is nevertheless the one that most contributes to our happiness in this world." From the article on "Christian Religion" in Denis Diderot and Jean le Rond d'Alembert, eds., *Encyclopédie, ou, dictionnaire raisonné des sciences, des arts et des métiers, par une société de gens de letters*. Paris: Chez Briasson, David, Le Bretton, Durand, 1751–1765. Vol. 14, 88.

36. In a famous essay of 1942, Benedetto Croce explained the relationship of Christianity not only with Europe but also with the whole world. "Christianity," he wrote, "was the greatest revolution ever experienced by humanity." He spoke of "Those geniuses of profound action, Jesus Christ, Paul, the author of the fourth Gospel, and the others who collaborated with them in various ways during the first Christian era," and of an "endless working–living and plastic–that would dominate the course of history." "Perché non possiamo non dirci cristiani," in *Discorsi di varia filosofia*. Bari: Laterza, 1945. 11.

37. Pope John Paul II, Apostolic Exhortation, *Ecclesia in Europa* (2003): "European culture gives the impression of 'silent apostasy' on the part of people who have all that they need and who live as if God does not exist" (article 9).

38. Gösta Hallonsten, "Verità e libertà," in *L'identità culturale dell'Europa,* ed. Paul Cardinal Poupard. Casale Monferrato, Italy: Piemme, 1994. 63.

39. George W. Bush, "The National Security Strategy of the United States of America," http://www.whitehouse.gov/nsc/nssall.html.

40. Ibid.

41. Ibid.

42. In his masterful conference of October 22, 2003, at the Institut d'Études Politiques in Paris, the Catalonian leader Jordi Pujol, "a European patriot," as he describes himself, after having surveyed the history of the successes of Europe, which today is "the best social, economic, and political system in the world," and having listed its unresolved problems, asks, in relation to the European identity, "Why is Europe so afraid to speak of itself? Of its borders, its identity, its role in the world? To speak of itself and act accordingly?" *L'Europe à bout de souffle?* Barcelona: Generalitat de Catalunya, 2003. 21.

43. On the aggressive and non-reactive nature of the terrorist war on the West, Magdi Allam has written trenchantly in *Kamizaze made in Europe.* Milan: Mondadori, 2004. The toughest and most unflinching words on the subject have been written by Oriana Fallaci in her trilogy: *The Rage and the Pride.* New

York: Rizzoli, 2002; *The Force of Reason*. New York: Rizzoli, 2006; and "Oriana Fallaci Interviews Oriana Fallaci," distributed with *Corriere della Sera*, Milan, August 2004.

44. The idea of perpetual peace has led to Immanuel Kant being invoked more than any other philosopher both during and after the war in Iraq, also inappropriately. For Kant, perpetual peace is "an impracticable idea," even if "the political principles that are inclined toward this purpose, namely that serve to produce such alliances of states to bring populations closer to that goal, are not in fact unrealizable." This is because their purpose is to produce "a nearness to [the idea]," to "a task founded on duty and consequently on the rights of men and of states." Immanuel Kant, *Perpetual Peace and Other Essays on Politics, History, and Morals*. Indianapolis, Ind.: Hackett, 1983. Para. 61. According to Kant, until perpetual peace has been realized, a state does indeed have the right to wage war in the event of "first aggression" and of "prior [military] preparations that justify the right of *prevention* (*ius praeventionis*)." It also has this right in the event of a "simple increase of *power* (*potentia tremenda*) by another state that renders itself *frightening* (through the increase in its territory)." Para. 56.

45. J. F. Revel, *L'obsession anti-americaine*. Paris: Plon, 2002. 215.

46. The experts are divided on the nature of this war, and the literature is varied. Huntington (*Clash*) speaks of the "war of civilizations"; Paul Berman (*Terror and Liberalism*. New York: W.W. Norton, 2003) of another war against totalitarianism; J. Esposito (*The Islamic Threat*) of a "clash of interests"; and others offer still different theories. Michael Mandelbaum, for example, considers the September 11 terrorist attacks as stumbling blocks in the whig theory of history that prevailed on the threshold of the twenty-first century: "However much the September 11 attacks may have aimed to strike the heart of the international order," he writes, "their effect was closer to that of an unpleasant experience in which you stumble and fall violently to the ground." *The Ideas That Conquered the World: Peace, Democracy, and Free Markets in the Twenty-First Century*. New York: PublicAffairs, 2002.

47. Pietro Citati, "L'Occidente senza forza e l'esercito del terrore." *La Repubblica*, March 31, 2004.

48. Mario Vargas Llosa, "L'Occidente. L'agonia del paradiso." *La Stampa*, April 18, 2004.

49. Ibid.

NOTES TO
The Spiritual Roots of Europe:
Yesterday, Today, and Tomorrow

1. Herodotus, *The History*, trans. David Grene. Chicago: University of Chicago Press, 1987. I, 4.

2. For a perceptive, broad view of the formation of Europe as both a place and a value, see Peter Brown, *The Rise of Western Christianity: Triumph and Diversity, 200–1000 AD*. Oxford: B. H. Blackwell, 1996.

3. See Helmut Gollwitzer, "Europa, Abendland," *Historisches Wörterbuch der Philosophie*, vol. 2, ed. J. Ritter. Basel: Schwabe, 1971. 824–26; Friedrich Prinz, *Von Konstantin su Karl dem Großen*. Düsseldorf: Artemis und Winckler, 2000.

4. Gollwitzer, "Europa, Abendland," 826.

5. Of the rich and varied literature on monasticism, two essential works I would indicate are: Hugo Fischer, *Die Geburt des westlichen Zivilisation aus dem Geist des romanischen Mönchtums*. Munich: Kösel, 1969; and Friedrich Prinz, *Askese und Kultur. Vor- und frühbenediktinisches Mönchtum an der Wiege Europas*. Munich: Beck, 1980.

6. Endre von Ivánka, *Rhömaerreich und Gottesvolk*. Freiburg-Munich: K. Alber, 1968.

7. Documentation and literature can be found in U. Duchrow, *Christenheit und Weltverantwortung*. Stuttgart: Klett, 1970. 328 ff. Complete documentation is available in Hugo Rahner, *Abendländische Kirchenfreiheit; Dokumente über Kirche und Staat in frühen Christentum*. Einsiedeln, Köln: Verlagsanstalt Benziger, 1943. Stephan Horn indicated to me an important text of Pope Leo the Great, contained in the pope's letter to the emperor of May 22, 452, in which he rejects the famous canon 28 of Chalcedon (on Constantinople's primacy over Rome, based on the location of the emperor's seat in the former): *"Habeat sicut optamus Constantinopolitana civitas gloriam suam, et protegente Dei dextera diuturno clementiae vestrae fruatur imperio, alia tamen ratio est rerum saecularium alia divinarum, nec praeter illam petram quam Dominus in fundamento posuit stabilis erit ulla constructio"* (LME II [37] 55, 52–56; cfr. ACO II/IV S. 56). On this issue, see also A. Michel, "Der Kampf um das politische oder petrinische Prinzip der Kirchenführung," in A. Grillmeier and H. Bacht, *Das Konzil von Chalkedon*, vol. 2, *Entscheidung um Chalkedon*. Würzburg: Echter, 1953. 491–562. Also the essay by Thomas O. Martin on canon 28 of Chalcedon in the same volume (433–458).

8. Otto Hiltbrunner, *Kleines Lexicon der Antike*. Bern-München: Francke, 1950. 102.

9. Although the Italian word *laico* shares with the English "lay" the primary meaning of non-clerical and the secondary meaning of non-professional, in religious discourse it also refers to non-believers, who could be variously rendered as agnostics, or secular people. In political discourse it has a long and complicated history in Italy owing to its association with the main opposition parties during the period in which the Christian Democrats governed the country. –Translator's note.

10. Arnold Joseph Toynbee. *A Study of History: Abridgement of Volumes I–VI,* Ed. D. C. Somerwell. New York: Oxford University Press, Reprint edition, 1987. Originally published 1947–1957. 276. Quoted from J. Holdt, *Hugo Rahner: Sein geschichtstheologisches Denken.* Schöning: Paderborn, 1997. 53. The paragraph "Philosophische Besinnung auf das Abendland" (52–61) offers particularly important material on the question of Europe.

11. Oswald Spengler, *The Decline of the West,* trans. Charles Francis Atkinson. New York: Knopf, 1957. For a discussion of the disputes over his thesis, see the chapter "Die abdendländische Bewegung zwichen den Weltkriegen," in Holdt, *Hugo Rahner,* 13–17. Comparison to Spengler is also a constant motif of Theodor Steinbüchel's fundamental works

on moral philosophy in the period between the two wars, *Die philosophische Grundlegung der katholischen Sittenlehre,* 2d ed. Düsseldorf: Schwann, 1947. First edition 1938.

12. Holdt, *Hugo Rahner,* 54.

13. The obligatory reference here is to the following words of Erwin Chargaff: "Where everyone is free to play the lion's part—in the free market, for example—what is attained is the society of Marsyas, a society of bleeding cadavers." *Ein zweites Leben. Autobiographische und andere Texte.* Stuttgart: Klett-Cotta, 1955. 168.

14. G. Hirsch, "Ein Bekenntnis zu den Grundwerten." *Frankfurter Allgemeine Zeitung,* October 12, 2000.

NOTES TO
Letter to Joseph Ratzinger

1. Aristotle, *Nicomachean Ethics,* trans. David Ross. New York: Oxford University Press, 1984. III.3, 1112b11.

NOTES TO
Letter to Marcello Pera

1. See Translator's note (note 9) in "The Spiritual Roots of Europe: Yesterday, Today, and Tomorrow" in this book. –Translator's note.

Index of Names